Advance Praise for *On Wholeness*

"Suffused with the 'living memory' of Anishinaabeg, Quill Christie-Peters's *On Wholeness* is poetry and critique, manifesto and philosophy. It feels both timeless and deeply attuned to the realities of Indigenous peoples in Canada and those of our 'global relations.' Most urgently, Christie-Peters demonstrates with wisdom and love that we can imagine and enact a world beyond the depravities of the colonial present."
—Billy-Ray Belcourt, author of *Coexistence* and *A Minor Chorus*

"I seem to have been waiting for this book all my life. I cried. I laughed. I was filled with awe. Quill Christie-Peters's voice is vital, and the messages that spill out of this book are timely reminders of what it means to be whole, to be connected to land and others, and to be alive. While reading, I felt my being expand and my heart radiate against my ribcage. I am so grateful for Quill Christie-Peters's voice."
—Helen Knott, author of *Becoming a Matriarch*

"Quill Christie-Peters's *On Wholeness* is an emotional and spiritual journey of liberatory embodiment. Quill's fleshy Anishinaabe values are deployed to tackle some of the stickiest aspects of motherhood, working in institutions, sovereign projects, and settler colonialism. Through our bodies, dreams are manifest and a spiritual wholeness becomes possible. You will both be changed and desire change after reading."
—Wanda Nanibush, Anishinaabe writer/curator

On Wholeness

On Wholeness

ANISHINAABE PATHWAYS
TO EMBODIMENT AND
COLLECTIVE LIBERATION

Quill Christie-Peters

AMBROSIA

Published in Canada and the USA in 2025 by House of Anansi Press Inc.
houseofanansi.com

29 28 27 26 25   1 2 3 4 5

Library and Archives Canada Cataloguing in Publication
Title: On wholeness : Anishinaabe pathways to embodiment and collective liberation / Quill Christie-Peters.
Names: Christie-Peters, Quill, author
Identifiers: Canadiana (print) 20250252988 | Canadiana (ebook) 20250253224 | ISBN 9781487013257 (softcover) | ISBN 9781487013264 (EPUB)
Subjects: LCSH: Mind and body. | LCSH: Human body (Philosophy) | LCSH: Human body—Social aspects. | LCSH: Settler colonialism. | LCSH: Decolonization.
Classification: LCC BF161 .C57 2025 | DDC 128/.2—dc23

Cover design: Alysia Shewchuk
Cover artwork: Quill Christie-Peters
Interior design and typesetting: Lucia Kim

House of Anansi Press is grateful for the privilege to work on and create from the Traditional Territory of many Nations, including the Anishinabeg, the Wendat, and the Haudenosaunee, as well as the Treaty Lands of the Mississaugas of the Credit.

With the participation of the Government of Canada
Avec la participation du gouvernement du Canada

We acknowledge for their financial support of our publishing program the Canada Council for the Arts, the Ontario Arts Council, and the Government of Canada.

Printed and bound in Canada

*For my late Grandpa Harry, and all the futures of
wholeness that will descend from him*

*And for my daughter, Giizik, who holds us in
the certainty of those beautiful futures*

Contents

PART II

She is full like the moon, rupturing like a galaxy and dancing with her ancestors like smoke rising to the sky

I am sitting in a bustling café with my back pressed firmly against a hard bench. I am only thirty-one years old, yet it feels so hard to keep my back upright in this weighted world. The bench beneath me is hard and angular against my soft flesh—the juxtaposition of my tender Anishinaabe existence against the unforgiving settler colonial world. I have worked so hard to stay soft. We have worked so hard to stay soft—generations upon generations of Anishinaabeg working to stay soft like the moss bogs of our homelands that seep water to rupture the concrete roads that traverse us. Under the gentle moonlight, I have kneaded my body like warm dough in order to retain its supple roundness—my edge is infinite.

A healer once told me that my shoulders want to round in order to protect my heart, and I imagine my centre like a whirlpool, pulling my body into the sacred smoke of my swirling chest so that I might become a magenta eddy of stardust and cosmic dust. If I close my eyes tight enough, I can feel myself floating softly through pink galaxies. If I focus hard enough, I can recede so far into my own body that I emerge in the great beyond, the place where my ancestors dance omnipresently and with an absolution unbounded by time and space. If I take a slow breath, my eyes closed, I can feel the swirling smoke inside my body, the low moan of creation expelling the expansive, dancing universe in each steady breath.

Our Anishinaabe bodies, wild and shifting with the pulse of the universe, flicker between many states. Sometimes, we are simply human beings delighting in our earthly experiences. Sometimes, we are joined by ancestors who sing through our flesh. Sometimes our feet are planted firmly on earth, and sometimes our feet dance upon stars. We are always everything all at once, a reality incomprehensible to the linearity of the settler colonial world. Even as a child I carried this inherent knowing, a seed planted deep into bone and watered tenderly by generations of Anishinaabeg fighting to persist, with softness.

Despite the swirling smoke deep within my chest, I have not always been present enough to receive it. My body has not always been soft enough to feel its discrepancy against a hard surface. At times, my body has been so hardened that its edges would meet the angular container of this bench with absolution, contained in its grasp. I have not always been able to tend to the wounds of my flesh, nor feel the embrace of the moon's light shining lovingly on my figure. It is during these times that my ancestors gather at the lip of the great beyond, where stardust begins to take shape into skin and bone, to sing me a simple song that calls me back into my body. It is during these times that they work tirelessly to warm my body, kneading my flesh back into supple flexibility so that the swirling smoke inside of my chest can ripple through my skin once again with the perpetual motion of creation. Here, creation is the throbbing pulse of existence, the infinite great mystery and the totality of the universe, earthbound and beyond. Creation loves our bodies so. My ancestors tend to my softness when I cannot. Our persistence has always been a collective endurance, even when enacted by our individual bodies.

My bones are timeless. They throb with the ethereal moans of my ancestors who congregate in their farthest corners, a dull and faint drumming. My bones are enduring. When my body one day decays, my bones will sink deep into the earth, returning to join the scaffolding of our mother, her primordial heartbeat pulsing with creation.

This book is an embodiment of Anishinaabe reality in all its fullness and complexity. I welcome you into my world, where my palms shimmer with stardust and my body dissolves back into the waterways and starscapes that birthed me. I welcome you into our world, which spans not only our earthly existence but far out into the great beyond, accessed through our beautiful, complex, wild, and shifting bodies. As Anishinaabe people, we use metaphor to communicate, teach, and relate to the world around us precisely because we live out these metaphors in our real and tangible lives. Much of the imagery in this book that describes what it means to exist beyond our physical bodies is not metaphor but lived reality for Anishinaabeg. When

I write, "She was full like the moon, rupturing like a galaxy and dancing with her ancestors like smoke rising to the sky," I mean it, literally and wholly. When I paint my ancestors gathering at the edge of my skin to build a fire that will call me back into my body despite the fragments, wounds, and losses, they are materially doing so.

To be Anishinaabe is to have the love of our ancestors viscerally transmitted to us in real time from the great beyond, through the body. To be Anishinaabe is to have stardust in our bones that echoes from the place in the sky that we come from and have responsibilities to. To be Anishinaabe is to be a drop of water in the flowing river of creation, held so tenderly by all our relations.

My blood is unbroken from the flow of the waterways I come from. Like a steady stream of water trickling over rock, the dark red hues of my mortality dance with the reverent rivers who birthed me. My blood is unbounded from the veins and channels that hold it. It also paints the starry night sky, red globular spheres floating through the constellations who breathed me into being.

I am a cisgender and able-bodied Anishinaabekwe with Scottish and Irish ancestors, visibly Native but not nearly as dark as many of my relatives. I grew up painting and writing. From the time I could hold a paintbrush, I envisioned futures informed by my ancestors' breath on a cold winter night, the mist of their voices rising to meet the stars. From the time I could write, my words traversed the place beyond time, the place before birth, the swirling smoke inside my own body, and the great beyond. Despite growing up with fragmented cultural immersion, I have always been irrevocably grounded in my identity as an Anishinaabe person through my worldview and the ways I have been resourced by my ancestors, the ways I have always danced with the swirling smoke inside me. When I received my Anishinaabe name, it all made so much sense. Kakekayatahseekobiik— never-ending light, that which we feel is lost resides in me. We are everything they can never contain. We are everything they can never reach. In a world of relentless settler colonial violence where so many Anishinaabe bodies are battered, bruised, and contorted under the weight of our intended destruction, we remain everything they can never be and everything they can never have. Our wild and flickering bodies innately evade their grasp from this world to the next. I have always known this.

Here on Turtle Island, settler colonialism has always been deeply terrified of Anishinaabe bodies and the swirling smoke inside of them. The settler colonial world, governed by the compartmentalization of life into discrete parts, which can then be used to generate hierarchy, seeks to solidify the structures of power that bolster colonial domination. Our bodies inherently evade these compartmentalizations. We flicker among many forms under the beating sun and shift into a smoke that is undefinable, incomprehensible, and untouchable to the colonial world, existentially and materially threatening the colonial project. As such, our bodies have always been the explicit target of the settler colonial state in both literal and metaphysical ways.

In the most literal sense, our bodies are removed from

the land through genocide and violence to ensure settler expansion and occupation. Here on Turtle Island, the older global settler colonies of Canada and the United States established themselves in the generations before us through widespread strategies of genocide such as massacres and forced starvation. Although these settler states work hard to frame these strategies as events that happened in the past, they are deeply rooted structures that persist in the present day, albeit obscured and enacted through more insidious forms of genocide cloaked in the discourse of reconciliation and inclusion. The settler state would have us believe that the attempted extermination of Indigenous peoples was a thing of the very distant past, but I only have to look to my father's generation for examples of this. The settler state would have us believe that they are working hard to take accountability for the mistakes of the past, but the collective experience of Indigenous peoples across Turtle Island says otherwise. We continue to experience forms of genocide that are intended to maintain an Indigenous population that is not threatening to the settler state and that destroy Indigenous bodies in a way that is not only tolerated but consented to by the larger population. They continue to do everything they can to remove our bodies from the land.

Our bodies are also targeted metaphysically as a way to weaken the ability of Indigenous peoples to resist our dispossession. This category of violence accounts for the otherwise unexplainably grotesque, perverted, and evil dimensions of settler colonial violence that explicitly target the relationship Indigenous peoples have with their own bodies and sense of self. On Turtle Island, Indigenous relationships to the

body have been targeted as a central colonial strategy—
from widespread sexual violence enacted on generations of
Indigenous peoples to the horrors of the residential school
system enacted on the bodies of our babies and children,
they have always tried to keep us from dancing with the
swirling smoke inside of us. Our bodies, and everything
they are capable of, terrify them so.

*My hair is celestial. Like the strands of web from a spider
weaving worlds, my hair tethers me to the galaxies that
swirl in the sky and in my heart. My hair is elusive. Its many
strands rise to the sky effortlessly and without gravity, the
web of body woven to the great beyond.*

Settler colonial disembodiment is one of the central
impacts of colonialism that Indigenous peoples must grapple
with in older settler colonies after generations of sustained
genocide. We experience disembodiment in multidirec-
tional ways that are birthed from places of both non-consent
and agency, but always through violence. Disembodiment
exists as both a violent orchestration by the settler colonial state in order to dispossess us and as a self-emanating
survival strategy that allows us to persist against all odds. I
speak back to the former. Not just the consequential harms
of our failed extermination, settler colonial disembodiment
is an intentional, sustained, and strategic limb of colonial
strategy that exists to suppress the ontological and material resistance of Indigenous embodiment. Settler colonial
disembodiment is the attempt to distance Indigenous self
from body, harming our bodies in such complex ways that

we must travel far away from them for our own survival and persistence. This disembodiment is multi-scalar—on the one end we might struggle to be present in our bodies to varying degrees, and on the other end we might walk away from our bodies permanently, leaving the earth to join our ancestors in the stars.

In an Anishinaabe worldview, disembodiment is much more than being removed from our physical bodies. By virtue of the swirling smoke inside of us and the ways we are woven into the web of creation around us, our bodies refuse to be compartmentalized to the physical realm. Our bodies are everything beyond the physical, traversing galaxy and earth, past and present—they are the holy containers of that beautiful swirling smoke that paints the universe around us. In alignment with our worldview that honours the expansive relationality that makes us whole, our bodies also encompass ancestor, homeland, star, and moon, forever flickering between many states. My body is the waterways of my homelands in Nezaadiikaang humming with the sounds of frogs and crickets, the pink galaxies that expelled me into body, and the way I access living ancestral archives. This is what Anishinaabeg have always celebrated—all our relations, embodied in the hub of our electric bodies that are rocked gently by the moon and held by the land.

Our wholeness requires us to experience presence within our bodies, but the ability to exist in a truly embodied state as an Indigenous person feels nearly impossible in a settler colonial world intent on the destruction of Indigenous life. Many of us do not live in a constant state of wholeness like our ancestors did but rather within varying degrees of disembodiment.

Many of us will continue to live in disembodiment. Many of us will continue to disembody ourselves as a survival strategy. Disembodiment, the creation of space between self and spirit from the body; sometimes it is all we can do so that we can breathe. Disembodiment, a result of incomplete genocide in which settler colonialism still attempts to remove our spirits from our bodies when it cannot physically remove our bodies from the earth itself. Disembodiment, the attempt to keep us from being whole, from swirling like smoke with our endless ancestors in the great beyond.

Importantly, to be whole is not some idealistic state of being that is free of pain and suffering. To be whole is simply to have access to all that we are and to be present enough, even if just momentarily, within our bodies so that we can feel our ancestors, homelands, and the great beyond pulsing within us. To be whole is a uniquely individual experience, and our bodies are so brilliant that they continue to find ways for us to be whole despite, and alongside, our disembodiment. I reject the binary of embodied/disembodied that would posit embodiment as an absolute end goal for wholeness and liberation, and disembodiment as a non-liberatory state of being. I reject the binary of embodied/disembodied that would discredit the ferocious swirling smoke within my relatives who rely on their disembodiment for survival. I instead embrace a nuanced understanding of what it means to experience presence within the Indigenous body that is wild, flickering, strategic, and celestial. To reclaim Anishinaabe embodiment is to find moments along the spectrum of disembodiment to dance with the swirling smoke inside of us—it is not absolute. To reclaim

Anishinaabe embodiment in the settler colonial world is to strategize how to grow closer to our inherent wholeness.

To be whole is our inherent right. It is also a vital part of our struggles for liberation from settler colonialism and imperialism. When we are whole, we are tethered firmly to our celestial responsibilities to build a more just world; we are resourced by our ancestors' care and knowledge; and we are able to materially fight for land, love, and body. Our collective liberation calls loudly for our wholeness.

Liberation is a large and lofty term. I define liberation as being complexly connected to my larger web of creation, which includes not only Anishinaabe people but all people, lands, and beings that are touched by the clutches of empire and imperialism that currently encase the globe. Liberation is nothing short of the full and total dismantling of this rusty and rotting structure of imperialism such that Indigenous peoples globally at last have the right to life. But if I narrow my scope to be more specific to the contents of this book, then liberation is also the right of all people, lands, and beings across the globe to be whole.

Whole, first and foremost, as in alive and here. Whole, then, as in able to experience presence within the body, perhaps delighting in the love and care their ancestors exude to them. Whole, as in not broken into disembodied pieces through relentless colonial and imperial violence. Whole, as in no parts of us have fallen off because they are too much to bear and too much to look at. Whole, as in no parts of us have been ripped off by the clutches of imperialism. Whole, as in soft, with no hardened edges sharpened by the acute violence on Indigenous bodies, lands, and waters.

Soft, as in flowing tenderly with the stream of creation that rocks our bodies in the tides of justice and goodness and purpose and joy. Soft, as in we can soften because we know we will live to watch our children grow up free and whole.

My flesh is so supple that the breath of a spirit can ripple its surface. My flesh is so soft that the land leaves imprints of itself on my body when it holds me. The stem and leaf of Labrador tea pressed into skin. My flesh is so flexible that it allows me to transform in the darkness of night, my body dissolving before my very eyes into my cosmic imprint, the low moan of creation.

I write this book at a time when the machinery of settler colonialism is being made visible at a scale and scope that has previously not been possible. Here on Turtle Island, tucked away in the older long-standing settler colony of Canada, I have borne witness to the escalation of genocide in Gaza by the younger settler colony of Israel, recognizing the experiences of my own ancestors in the people and children of Palestine. This moment in time is witnessed by so many.

My ancestors meet and embrace the martyrs of Palestine.

My ancestors bear witness to this genocide unfolding through the bodies of their descendants who shake with a shared rage that trembles across the great beyond. In the stillness of the night, my ancestors have whispered to me my responsibilities to build a world where Palestine is free. Our spirits bear witness to this genocide unfolding in the place beyond time, and even our most celestial entities have turned their heads toward the earth in response to the echoing of such immense violence across the universe. The smoke inside my chest swirls rapidly now as my ancestors act with urgency and our spirits huddle around the earth with concern. This moment has taught me so much about the spiritual dimensions of liberation, and how we are materially resourced through our wholeness to resist settler colonialism and imperialism. The ways in which I have been moved into action for Palestine touch all the words in this book.

My hands are so nimble. They craft words and worlds and hold babies and futures. They stroke hair and body and paint justice and wholeness. My hands are so tactile. They are meant to shape the world. My hands are so tired. They must shape the world.

I have only been in this body for thirty-one years, yet it already holds so many stories. This body has held me even when I could not love us back. I have lain in a curled heap on my bathroom floor many times. I have cried tears of pain and anguish, as well as tears of immeasurable happiness. I have opened my own flesh when times were hard, and I have opened the flesh of others to mark their bodies with the stardust of the great beyond. Inhabiting a body in the settler colonial world is always a complex contradiction. Despite my disembodiment, creation has always poured out of me. Despite our disembodiment, creation will always spill out of us.

As a cisgender, able-bodied Anishinaabe woman with a close proximity to whiteness through my mother, I hold privilege that has allowed me to experience a level of settler colonial violence and subsequent disembodiment that has harmed but not destroyed me. As an Anishinaabe artist, I have a responsibility to share how I creatively envision, dream, and make real my wholeness, particularly for my kin who cannot because of the scale of violence they experience. Even when I have not been able to be present in my body, I have been able to help others to be whole in theirs. Even in my darkest hours, I have never felt truly alone. Even when I have lain crumpled on my bathroom floor in despair, my tears have become an invocation for a beautiful future of wholeness and justice, smoke emanating from my chest in absolution.

Wholeness is our ability to continually return to, and visit with, the smoke inside us. To be whole is to be present enough in our bodies to viscerally feel all that they contain— the swirling smoke, the low moan of the universe, the love and care of all our ancestors who dance at the edge of skin. To be whole is to remember we are a part of the whole—an agentive and discrete being who is also cradled by many threads of creation that weave us within a larger web of responsibility and purpose that extends to us from the great beyond. To be whole is to remember our body is not just our physical form but also contains the smoke of the great beyond that accesses living knowledge from our ancestors, our spirits, and the celestial heartbeat of our existence. To be whole is to experience fleeting or permanent presence in our bodies, despite the pain, in order to live out our responsibilities that echo from the great beyond as calls for justice and liberation. The settler colonial world has always been terrified of this.

There are very specific moments in my waking life when I can feel the sensation of wholeness. Moments spent painting when I can feel my ancestors speaking to me through the colours that splash from my fingertips across canvas. The feeling of vibrant stillness and the suspension of time that surrounds our ceremonies. The hushed voices of spirits before I mark a body with ink and blood. The rupturing of my own body with blood and water to reach into the great beyond to birth my daughter. The feeling of my ancestors weeping beside me when they besieged Al-Shifa Hospital.

This book loosely mirrors my own creation story. In chapter 1, we begin in the place before body, the place before time, and the place before form, swirling like smoke with our ancestors in the great beyond. Here we understand wholeness as the ability to convene with all the elements of creation who hold us, and how ancestor, spirit, and homeland are woven into the fabric of our being, even beyond body and time.

In chapter 2, we are born into the settler colonial world. This chapter explores settler colonialism through the lens of its nuanced compartmentalizations that attempt to separate, make distinct, and ascribe value to our world in order to perpetuate power and control.

In chapter 3, I land in my specific body and discuss the ways in which settler colonialism has shaped it. I share my personal experiences of colonial harm to both situate the heart of my knowledge and signify its limits before explicitly exploring my own disembodiment in chapter 4.

After an interlude in which we return to the swirling smoke to remember all that our bodies hold, the chapters in part II chart my personal pathways to wholeness—what has taught me to be whole, what brings me closer to my body, and what allows me to dance with the sacred smoke inside me. These pathways are creative practice, parenting, pleasure, and infinite responsibility in relation to collective liberation. Witnessing the escalation of the genocide in Palestine in 2023 called me back into my body and taught me that wholeness is not just our right but is also our responsibility and methodology to deepen collective liberation.

Although I explore wholeness through the lens of my specific body and cultural identity as an Anishinaabe woman, I am writing not just for Anishinaabeg but for all who have been touched by imperialism and settler colonialism. When we are whole, we are resourced by our ancestors, held tenderly by the swell of creation, and better able to resist and transcend colonial violence. I hope my insistence on my own wholeness brings you closer to yours.

For our collective liberation.

PART I

Chapter 1

The place before body

My ancestors dance like swirling smoke across the vast night sky. In between pink galaxies and pockets of stars, they congregate in the natural eddies formed by the flowing sky of creation. Beyond our physical world, they are just like smoke—formless yet physical, fleeting yet permanent, discrete beings yet interconnected in ways beyond our comprehension. Sometimes, they are a whisper. Sometimes, they are clear in shape and form. Sometimes, they are a low moan reverberating throughout the vast plane of creation. Sometimes, they are a voice. Yet, always, swirling with ferocity and dancing like smoke within the endless sky.

In the place before birth, the place beyond time, the place before form, we all swirl like smoke. Without the confines of a body, we are like a whisper shooting across the sky, everything and nothing all at once. In the place before birth, our ancestors and spirit kin abound and we join them in the holy dance of creation, once again becoming ancestor and sighing in deep relief. Without body, we are also without time, and so we become thick like smoke, permeating all corners of the universe and churning through magenta galaxies punctuated with purple dust. Sometimes, we summon our form, but mostly we ebb and flow with the tides of the universe, releasing back into deep interconnection with all that we are and all that we will be, in fragile perpetuity. We live among the sound that is recorded from a black hole, a low moan echoing throughout the shifting universe. This sound is everywhere and everything and yet made up of many distinct voices that are agentive and alive. Without body and time, we are expansive beyond comprehension.

We are whole.

We are the whole.

My ancestors' bodies dissolve, particle by particle, with each exhalation of our infinite universe. Their blood mixes with stardust to create the magenta pigment that scatters the vast planes of the great beyond. Their hair is woven into the tender threads that tether our world to the next. Their hearts join the symphony of sounds that bounce off formless matter. They become smoke, disintegrated from their bodily forms into a sacred vapour that houses many worlds and many spirits. Sometimes, they take form. Sometimes, they are summoned. Like a winding river, the smoke descends through the star-scape to enter a single lodge. The smoke swirls inside the lodge, joining that of sage and tobacco that has been lit by the huddled bodies below.

The smoke of the great beyond is many things all at once. It is itself agentive and purposeful while also being the medium of creation in which individual entities may be called to take their discrete form. Out of the smoke come the clear voices of our ancestors, our spirits shown in flesh and physicality, and the smell of rushing fresh water. Anishinaabeg have always understood the smoke of the universe. It is a part of our living memory to remember and understand our relationship to the great beyond, and to ensure that this knowledge is passed down through generations. When we are in the place before body, we are the smoke, traversing galaxies with the flow of creation. When we are summoned to the place before birth, we sit with our ancestors and revel in the wholeness of being in complete interconnection with the universe around us. When we are born, we enter relatively rigid bodies, but as Anishinaabeg, we understand that the swirling smoke of creation also exists inside us. Housed within the physical confines of our new bodies, the smoke remains swirling wildly in our hearts. Our culture reflects this knowing, with many of our ceremonies and cultural practices oriented toward our ability to dance with the expanse of creation and swirl the smoke inside our bodies.

The smoke in the lodge carries the voices of familiar ancestors. In the darkness, their bodies materialize from the thick smoke to sit beside us. The hair on my arms rises to the sky. Sometimes, their voices are as clear and close as day. Other times, their voices sound like they are echoing from across the universe. The tail of an ancient spirit cuts the smoke with ferocity as it enters the lodge, bringing with it the humbling uneasiness of knowing that we sit at the precipice of the great beyond. In the lodge, we are whole.

The dissolving of our bodies, both into dirt and into stars, when we must one day leave them, does not render us shapeless or without agency. As flesh turns to earth and our familiarity decays, our imprint always remains. In the great beyond, every thread of our interconnection and every invocation of our creation is what retains our shape. In the great beyond, we remain the core of who we are through the specific ways we are tethered to creation through responsibility and kinship. Simultaneously, we exist as everything beyond ourselves, a delicate dance of self and other that is only made possible by the disintegration of time and space. As Anishinaabeg, we mirror this way of being, even in our earthbound bodies. We retain our ability to be many things all at once through the swirling smoke that is encased within the physical limitations of our bodies, allowing us to flicker between self and other. This has always been our way. Generations upon generations of Anishinaabeg have lived whole, tending to the sacred smoke within our bodies, traversing starscapes, and feeling the pulse of our homelands within our flesh.

In the great beyond, the stars are endless. Like expansive beadwork punctuating the darkness of non-matter, the stars sparkle and vibrate with the ancient hum of the universe. Manitou-man-eh-sug—beads rattling together—was the first sound, the low moan of creation that spoke into being all that we are and all that we will be. In a darkened lodge, silence is punctuated by the sound of a rattle, that same low moan of creation that calls forward the smoke.

The great beyond is endlessly overflowing with the motion of creation. It can never be stopped. It can never be quelled. Its exquisite and infinite expansion births realities that we can never truly grasp in our waking lives, but that we can deeply know and understand in our bodies, which are imprinted with the outlines of the constellations that we come from. The great beyond is many things all at once—a continuum of blurred creation, a matrix that suspends time and space, the place where spirits roam, and the place where our ancestors dance. The great beyond is many things all at once—the dull hum of a black hole, my body dissolving into stars, the parts of me that exist beyond body and time, our innate wholeness.

In the great beyond, our homelands are represented through the distinct spiritual beings that comprise them— water, copper, each individual tree, animal, plant, and being. Even in a relatively formless starscape characterized by infinite motion and sparkling stardust, place retains its significance. Even in an otherworldly matrix of unfamiliar sound and ancient visualizations, the land remains. The land persists beyond space and time because it is itself made up of spirits that tether themselves to both place and the great beyond. It is here where I start my self-location—in the great beyond, to credit the love and labour of near indescribable creation, ancestors, and spirit that work through Anishinaabeg so viscerally and make us who we are.

In a creation story told by my great-grandma, the great beyond is personified as a woman filling birch bark baskets with water from the river. Each basket is made of a different substance—ash and blood, the breath of a spider, the smoke of creation. Each basket is impermanent and begins to rupture with small holes that eventually burst, yet she continues to fill them diligently. Each basket is a thing born or dying within the spectrum of life. Her body itself is filled with the swirling river of creation. Sometimes, serpents and turtles congregate in her head, which swells like a balloon filling with water until her bulbous head finally overflows and rolls down her body, representing a time where certain creatures set the tone of the universe.

I gaze upon my great-grandparents in the great beyond as a vibrant mass of stars surrounded by pink hues that dance across the sky. Their breath makes the stars sing. Their breath blows magenta dust across the universe like wind across ancient sand dunes. In my world, they were known as Agnes Wayash and Pete Kabatay, strong, hard-working, and intelligent Anishinaabeg who fought so hard for the survival of their descendants. I never got to meet them, but I glimpse them through my father, who was raised by them deep in the bush, and through my grandmother, who keeps their stories and knowledge alive in every moment of every day. I never got to know them in my waking life, yet I know them. My great-grandpa Pete's helper was the bear, and the bear came to me when I was young—consistently, unfaltering, and overt. One day those bears came to me in a dream and showed me the pink galaxies that my daughter would descend from. I think of my great-grandpa's joyous celestial smile as he sang those bears down from the stars to reach me.

I gaze upon my great-great-grandmother in the place before body as the corridors and pathways that snake across many galaxies to connect worlds through light and energy. She was just eight years old when she survived the massacre of her entire family by hiding under their dead bodies. I think of what she endured, only to witness, through the wailing grief of her descendant—a grief so intense that it surely reached the galaxies she is a part of—the same story of such immense violence in Hind Rajab, the six-year-old Palestinian girl who was murdered alongside her family. My great-great-grandmother survived, but Hind Rajab did not. Hearing her descendants' otherworldly cries, she transformed herself into a starlit corridor to connect our ancestors with Palestinian martyrs, wrapping them in our celestial love. I like to imagine that my great-great-grandmother was able to embrace Hind momentarily in the great beyond, and through their embrace, Anishinaabeg and Palestinian futures became even more irrevocably intertwined.

I gaze upon my paternal grandfather in the place beyond time as a comet lighting up the dark night sky. He drowned at Lac des Mille Lacs when my father was just an infant. In the great beyond, I find my grandfather and hold him gently in my arms because our grief can still ripple through the threads of creation, especially when we leave our babies too soon. I think of all the times I have waded into that lake and imagined his body dissolving back into our boggy homeland, hoping that my body swimming in those same waters would echo into the great beyond and make him smile. On that same shore, in a different moment, my young grandmother waited anxiously with her firstborn son, my father, in her arms. Finally, she had no choice but to walk into town in complete uncertainty. As she did, a comet fell across the sky, briefly illuminating her infant son's eyes with the light of the great beyond.

I gaze upon my maternal grandmother, Peggy Cade, in the great beyond, where she exists simply as infinity. She is everywhere and nowhere, everything and nothing—too big for me to even comprehend. After we lost my grandma, I once had a vivid lucid dream where I desperately tried to find my grandmother hiding in the corners of my dreams, but I could not, and I woke up sobbing and screaming her name. After she passed, I felt like she was a shooting star that was called to the farthest corners of the universe. Not even a whisper of her remained. I sometimes wonder if I don't feel her in the same way that I do my Anishinaabe ancestors because she was Irish and perhaps had different places to be. But I think the real answer is that she was always an infinite light too big for this universe, even in her earthbound body. With my eyes fixed on the night sky, my face is warmed by a shooting star for a fleeting moment—oh, to be graced by a spirit so divine.

I gaze upon my maternal grandfather, Harry Christie, who made his journey just as I was finishing this book, as the vibrant and reliable sun emitting rays of bright orange light that warm my face on the earth that feels so changed now that he is gone. I close my eyes on a sunny spring day and feel his love that was always so steady, so sturdy, even when there was distance between us. Look, now, at how the flowers love you so. You warm their petals and the birds begin to sing. Look, now, at how the waters rejoice in your shimmer. Look, now, at my face and how it softens in the sunlight when I think of how much I love you. He now becomes the sun, in tender relief after his earthbound existence, to be held by the love he could not always receive but that was always there, in absolution. And as the sun shines, it finds itself held by infinity. My grandmother meets my grandfather in the great beyond—the infinite expanse of her being met with the everlasting rays of the glorious sun. On a night where I feel like my heart might actually break open, I hear my grandmother whisper my name and I know I am held by them both at this moment.

I gaze upon the relatives I have known in my waking life who were taken from the earth too soon. I see my late auntie Norma in the great beyond as the ever-watchful moon. She rests in the holy embrace of dibiki-giizis, and they both watch over me with adoration. She always loved so deeply and with such radical kindness, her face wrinkling up into a goofy grin that was an anchor for our persistence across generations. I see my late uncle Steve in the great beyond as a blue constellation that emanates peace. He was my father's other half. They survived residential school by laughing deep into their bellies together. I see my late cousin Darren shining away in the farthest corner of the great beyond, a bright and sturdy star. I see him as a distant star because his light is so bright—only the strongest of spirits could endure what he did. I gaze upon my first dog, and soulmate, Sky, in the great beyond as the shimmer of stardust that punctuates the galaxies containing all our beautiful ancestors. He was my saviour, my best friend, and the one who helped me survive. When I named my daughter Sky, I knew that the great beyond shimmered with vibrancy.

My self-location starts in the great beyond and extends far beyond my human relations. Niibi—our first mother, the conductor of all creation—flows like a rushing river throughout the place before body. Through her, we look directly into the stars. Through her, we are taught that our bodies are a reflection of the beautiful and expansive universe, and that we have everything we need inside our bodies. Mukwa—bear—speaks to us so clearly and appears on my thighs in ink and blood to commit me to a future where my children can live free on their homelands. Ozaawaabiik—copper, keeper of our relatives and conduit to different worlds—shines brightly in rock and in galaxy, an embodiment of the dimensionality of Anishinaabe existence.

In the place beyond body, we are held by so many. Our knowledge comes from so many.

In the lodge, my body vibrates with the hum of creation, and with each laboured breath, I exhale all that I am, and my body follows. I cough out a tree frog who disappears into the rocks, and I feel my ancestors braiding my hair, tethering me to all that I will be. I am the smoke now. A bear's muffled grunting. The sound of a black hole.

In the great beyond, I am fully dissolved into smoke. My form is now contained within the threads of communion that traverse this world and into the next. I am everything and nothing and everything in between. Still the heart of who I have always been; beyond my body, I am a soft but firm imprint visible to the cosmic gaze. Beside me, and within me, I feel the wind from a thunderbird's wing rippling stardust and water, the warmth from a bear who has joined me, and the presence of many whom words simply cannot hold. I am past and future, gazing upon my ancestors while tending to my descendants, all while wrapped within the love and care of creation unfolding.

But now, it is time to travel to the edge of time. The smoke I am a part of moves like a slow, winding river across the cosmic planes to make its way to the place before birth, thickening at the precipice of a world beyond.

We gather at the place before birth with our ancestors and spirit kin when we are ready to descend back into body. Our ancestors materialize out of the smoke to bear witness to another cycle. Our spirits come to enact their responsibilities to weave worlds together. As we assume form, we begin to feel our bodies being woven from the fabric of our homelands and the familiar chatter of our ancestors beside us. All my beautiful ancestors are surrounding me now, flickering between their celestial and earthly forms.

At the edge of time, the precipice of body, the place before birth, I gaze down at my life and consent to it. I feel myself thicken out of the smoke, many voices around me now, and the threads that hold me begin to weave into material form. I am sitting with them now—the sounds of beads rattling, ancient voices, primordial rumblings. All my loving ancestors, all the spirits who care for Anishinaabeg, all of creation, have congregated at the place before birth, joined by the holy spider to weave spirit to earth. With wrinkled faces of cosmic joy and unending hope, they all start to weave me into body as I begin to descend out of the stars.

Chapter 2

To be born in this world
Settler colonial compartmentalization

In the womb, our body is sustained by a complex mass of vessel and vein, weaving our flesh within the body of our parent and to the great beyond. In the womb, our soft bodies take shape with tendrils of web extending to the place before birth. Taught by the spider, we flicker between this world and the others, using our webs to traverse time and space. During this time, the spider works tirelessly to build a sturdy web so that we may be bound to the great beyond as children. When it is our time to be born, the spider smiles and dissolves into stardust. The web remains.

With great pressure and the heavy weight of a new-found physicality, we are born into our bodies and take our first breath. Feeling the tension of our skin holding form, the comforting rhythm of our new breath, the gentle restriction of our movement through gravity, the body binds us to the earth while cradling us within the larger web of creation. When we are babies, the boundaries between our body and our parents' bodies are blurred, the skin between us melt-ing from the waves of otherworldly love that lapse on its shore. When we are children, the spider still watches over us intently, guarding the sacred web that weaves us to the great beyond as we flicker between many worlds. As we get older, the web dissolves and our feet become firmly planted on the earth. But always, the swirling smoke remains within our bodies and connects us to everything that we are. As we grow older still, we learn to use ceremony and art to visit with that swirling smoke and to continue dancing with the great beyond. Anishinaabe bodies have always been wild like smoke. Even in our earthbound bodies, we insist on spilling over them in reverence for our expansive web of creation.

From an Anishinaabe understanding, the body is not just the physical vessel. The smoke is thick inside of us, and so our bodies also contain our ancestors, homelands, and the great beyond. Our bodies are the containers of linear time and space, yet our bodies are also the way in which we exit those confines to dance with our ancestors. Our bodies are contained by flesh and blood, bone and marrow, but this containment also holds space for the sacred swirling smoke within us, the dull hum of the universe reverberating with every pump of our heart. At the edge of our skin, our ancestors visit us with stories that will guide us to a more just future. Within our hot blood, the swift currents of our waterways hum to us through its rapids. Our bodies are every single strand of creation we are embedded within, the threads of our existence woven by the loving hands of our ancestors in the great beyond.

To have a body is to feel tension. The tension of skin stretching

over bone and muscle. If the body ruptures, red blood pours
out with the voices of ten thousand ancestors who live inside
us. To have a body is to feel gentle containment. The breath,
an anchor to our individuality. The form, a reminder of our
fleeting existence. The bones, carriers of earth. If we rupture,
one million stories, everlasting galaxies, past, present, and
future, rush out of the body in one flowing river.

The containment and tensions that maintain our physical bodies on earth are gentle and tender—skin and bone,
memory and hair, and the swirling smoke of the universe
deep inside it all. We are held within the here and now by
our soft and temporary flesh—our bodies, the vessel of our
human experience that is delicately fleeting. The finality of
time in this life holds only so much power when we know
we will return to the place beyond time. The deterioration
of body is like being carried down a stream that, bit by bit,
will dissolve us back into creation.

There is great joy in the limitations and specific experiences that come from having a body. We delight in the
fleeting spectrum of emotions our bodies afford us—love,
grief, loss, connection, and movement mark our bounded
and private experience containerized by the body. And
although so much of our individual experience feels private,
we are simultaneously held by so many. The spider gazes
upon us lovingly as we grow old, ready to extend its web
so we can climb back up to the stars when it is our time to
return to the great beyond.

However, unlike the gentle containment of our spirits
within our physical bodies, Indigenous people must contend

with the external containment of our wild and flickering bodies cemented by settler colonial violence and force. When we are born, we do not just land in our beautiful bodies; we also land in a settler colonial world intent on the destruction of Indigenous life. Some of us confront settler colonial violence as soon as we are born, removed from our loving parents' arms shortly after we've taken our first breath. Some of us are eased into the world of rigidity, violence, and control that immerses our bodies, coming to quickly understand our intended destruction as small children.

The containment of our bodies is no longer tender with the embrace of skin and bone around spirit; it is unnatural and suffocating as the structures of settler colonialism surround us. Here, our bodies become stretched thin like skin over too much bone. Here, our bodies lose their movement and fluidity, like a vibrating orb contained within a rigid box. Here, our bodies carry so much weight that if we falter for just one moment, we risk being flattened completely. From birth, we must contend with the razor-sharp violence of settler colonialism.

Settler colonialism is ultimately a project of rigidity, violence, and control. Although there are many ways to define settler colonialism, in the most fundamental sense it is the removal of Indigenous bodies from their homelands in order to clear the land for settler occupation and capitalist expansion. I use the term *body* in this definition not to diminish the personhood of Indigenous peoples but rather to emphasize the Anishinaabe understanding of personhood, which innately includes within our bodies our ancestors, homelands, and all of creation. On Turtle Island, settlers seek to reside in the place that they have invaded, creating an unquestionable impetus for the ongoing removal of Indigenous bodies from their homelands. By necessity, settler colonialism must be structural, sustained in every moment of every day. Here on Turtle Island, Indigenous peoples have persisted for generations through multi-faceted forms of genocide and dispossession. From outright massacres, biowarfare, forced starvation, residential schools, and relocation through the reserve system to the present era of so-called reconciliation and Indigenization forwarded by settler institutions, the many forms of violence required to maintain the colonial relationship proliferate. Although these strategies are more obscured now, Indigenous peoples continue to live through genocide and dispossession while the neo-settler colony of Canada weaponizes a false ethic of apology and change as the newest frontier of our insidious destruction.

If we could imagine the Indigenous world before settler colonialism, we might gaze upon a relationality that is unfathomable in its expansiveness. If we could imagine creation unscathed by settler colonialism, we might envision a river flowing fiercely with interconnection, flux, and fluidity. This river flows over our homelands, rushing with the ferocity of the pulse of the great beyond and bringing together all the relations of the land and beyond. This river inherently evades rigidity—its expansiveness and connectivity the antithesis to control and hierarchy. Creation terrifies settler colonialism because it transcends the logics and requirements of the settler colonial world effortlessly and without pause. Indeed, it is the power of this river that forms continuous cracks in the concrete walls of colonialism— cracks that sometimes burst, letting the river assume its wild form momentarily; cracks that will one day obliterate these walls completely.

Settler colonialism imposes itself over top of the flowing stream of creation inherent to Anishinaabe homelands. It must quell the flow of creation that inherently spills over the boundaries and hierarchies that colonialism works so hard to maintain. It also necessitates stagnancy and solidification in order to control the wild, rushing, and transcendent flow of creation that continually births life, love, and relation beyond oppression.

First, settler colonialism does what it can to diminish the contents of the river itself—committing genocide against not just the bodies of Indigenous peoples but also all of our relations—the fish, bear, tree, manoomin. To control the rushing river, settler colonialism erects dams and blockages to stop the flow of water, with the eventual goal of separating it completely into discrete pools that can no longer reach one another. This represents the central scaffolding of the settler colonial project—harsh lines, boxes, boundaries, and borders—compartmentalizations that attempt to separate and control the multi-faceted components of creation that are always dancing together in complicated motion.

My dad tells me that we never used to have a word in our language for hello. We didn't think of ourselves as discrete enough to warrant a greeting that signified the separation of self from another in that way. Rather, it was like we were

*all particles in a stream—individual in our embodiment but
flowing together wildly within the river of creation.*

The central scaffolding of compartmentalization must
exist prior to the establishment of the larger structures
of oppression that solidify colonial domination—it is the
groundwork, foundation, and invisibilized necessity of the
colonial project. In order to manufacture power in the first
place, the complex web of creation, or the rushing river,
must be separated into pieces that are rendered distinct
from one another and removed from their relationality.
Only when pieces of creation are considered to be separate
can they then be prescribed value to generate hierarchy.
Compartmentalization of the entirety of Indigenous life,
land, and body is the prerequisite to hierarchy and the
generation of power, and thus stands as the ontological
backbone of the settler colonial project. Containment and
rigidity hold the entire system in place. Settler colonialism
does everything it can to control the ferocity of movement
and interconnection that is inherent to creation.

On Turtle Island, the physical architecture of settler colonialism has been established to root its scaffolding within
earth and body. This architecture reflects the compartmentalization that is the central structuring logic of settler
colonialism. The rocks that contain our ancient relatives
were blasted with dynamite to carve out harsh and linear
railways and roads. Our waterways full of life and sponta-
neity were blocked with concrete dams, and now the land
holds the tears of the river. Farmlands composed of mono-
culture grids span endlessly across the prairies. Pipelines

shoot sharp lines deep into the earth and bleed death. Cities made up of box-shaped skyscrapers punctuate the skylines, and little box-like houses litter the land to keep the nuclear family separated from all else. Our trees are logged in huge clumps, forming compartments across the land hidden from the view of highways and roads. All around us—harsh lines, boxes, and a stifling of the inherent movement of creation.

But, and always, in a world of rigidity and control, Indigenous bodies still pulse with the sweetness of infinite creation as the smoke swirls within our chests. The undefinability and flux of our bodies poses a fundamental threat to the settler colonial world.

The wild and flickering body of my great-great-grandfather. At the same time that they laid down roads on the weeping land, blasting rock and flooding our waterways with dams, my great-great-grandfather laid his expansive body to rest on the angular and harsh lines of the railway tracks. His body, separated into pieces by the force of the train, suffered the same fate as our homelands. I imagine, as he was separated, that his body erupted into wisps of stardust and sputtered out a green frog and blooming flowers that sang a beautiful song for his journey under the moonlight. Even in our death, we are many things. Even in our most literal forms of separation, we are everything all at once.

The physical architecture of settler colonialism separates the land, and all its inherent creation, into bits and pieces. The rushing river is slowed and the land is marked off into discrete boxes that we can see from the sky. The expansive land becomes littered with borders and roads that control the movement of bodies, animals, and beings. The more finite architecture of colonialism—the nuts and bolts—is intricate containerization and compartmentalization that cascades to restrict all facets of our existence. On top of the rigid scaffolding of lines and boxes, the architects must build systems of compartmentalization that are multi-scalar, attempting to hold our shifting and wild bodies in place all the way from our environment to our inner selves.

The flow of creation must be bounded and static in order to create the building blocks of settler colonialism. The flow of creation must be categorized, defined, compartmentalized, and contained as the prerequisite to power. Hierarchy simply cannot be generated without discrete units to place above or below one another, and hierarchy is the backbone of power. The ontological foundation of settler colonialism, and both its crude and finite architecture, is the compartmentalization of life and the construction of the system of value that informs how those compartments stand alongside, or atop, one another.

The compartmentalization of the settler colonial world must be all-encompassing and layered, with the swell of creation and the wild and flickering bodies of Indigenous peoples always threatening to burst the seams of the colonial project, spilling out the rushing river in glorious triumph. This compartmentalization is also deeply invisibilized, taking root even below the already naturalized structures of power we seek to transcend. In the most metaphysical sense, one of the foundational compartmentalizations of settler colonialism is the attempted separation of body from land, ancestor, spirit, and all of creation. Stated differently, colonialism attempts to separate each individual from the flow of creation they exist within. From the restriction of our expansive expressions of gender and sexuality to a binary system of cisgender woman or man; from the restriction of our extended community structures to the nuclear family, compartmentalization is the fundamental necessity of settler colonialism that reaches into all facets of our lives.

In the settler colonial world, the individual is separate from the collective, the child is separate from the parent, our art is separate from life, and our bodies are separate from our homelands. And within these separations, value is prescribed in accordance with settler colonial conceptions of power. Land is considered less valuable than body, ancestor less than self, and child less than parent. In the felt sense, the compartmentalization of settler colonial life is profoundly lonely, a project of ultimate isolation and removal from our inherent interconnections.

My body is soft and tender, pulled in many directions and stretched thin. Across the dimpled flesh of a thigh, an unnatural line marking a boundary that should not dare to exist. Even our birch bark baskets that are meant to hold and contain have loose tops where berries and medicines can spill out. Even our bodies that are meant to contain our spirits can rupture with blood and water to bring our babies down from the stars. Even our beadwork, fastened so tightly with thread, is meant to one day break loose. Across my body traverse long roads, metal railways, and deep holes where the spirits are supposed to live—the place on our territory where a big piece of rock was blasted with dynamite for a road. My grandmother told me that as long as that rock is not whole, then neither are we. "Tell your grandchildren," she said.

The process of differentiating, separating, and categorizing creation is very different from honouring the natural distinctions and differences inherent within creation. As Anishinaabe people, we celebrate the differences and diversity within our web of relationality as a central tenet of creation itself. We are able to hold ourselves as individual beings while basking in the ways we are a part of the deep relationality around us. The processes of compartmentalization that settler colonialism relies on reject relationality in order to containerize and isolate pieces of creation from one another. This distinguishment and separation denies the interconnection between realities, effectively un-relating entities from one another.

The disconnection that comes from this compartmentalization is essential for assigning a system of value. When the world is interconnected, it is impossible to ascribe value to one element of this interconnection without it spilling onto others. Only once the world is rendered into discrete entities can individual value be ascribed to those entities. From here, this imposed system of value can generate the hierarchies that form the structures of oppression we are familiar with in settler colonial society—ableism, ageism, cisheteropatriarchy, capitalism, and white supremacy, to name a few.

Although an interrogation of settler colonial compartmentalization must be intersectional in order to account for the scale and connectivity of these structures of oppression, it is helpful to start with the body as a central hub for the compartmentalizing grasp of settler colonialism. In the settler colonial world, the body is compartmentalized to just the physical. Removed from the homelands that the body belongs to, removed from the ancestors that ushered that body into existence, removed from the pulse of the ever-shifting universe, the body is simply flesh and bone. The body is static, firmly planted in linear space and time. The memory of the body extends to the living relatives who shape it—parents and grandparents—but not beyond. To care for the body, we fix its physical ailments. To feel pleasure, we can only imagine physical and individualized pleasure. The body is a mere vessel—empty, physical, and removed from the inherent wholeness of all that we are.

In contrast, the Anishinaabe body is full and whole. Through our bodies, we dance with our ancestors, access internal knowledge from the great beyond, and feel our homelands in our veins. We spill over the boundaries that attempt to remove body from ancestor, spirits, and the great beyond. We tend to the smoke inside of us that rises back up to the stars that we come from.

The colonial compartmentalization of the body to the physical realm funnels us toward the precedence of the individual. Rather than a conception of the individual as a unique being, the individual in the settler colonial context is absolute, without collective responsibility, and at the top of the hierarchy. Removed from the expansive relationality housed within the body, the individual is also removed from their codependency with the elements of creation around

them, generating an individualized relationship to responsibility. The individual becomes the unit of capitalism, unable
to rely on the world around them for their well-being and
oriented instead toward their own individualistic prosperity
that is allocated by the system of capitalism.

In the settler colonial world, the individual lives in a
singular and static body. At most, their responsibility extends
to the nuclear family, petering out at the edges of extended
family. Compartmentalized from their ancestors, the individual is removed from generations of knowledge and care
related to worldbuilding, instead relying on external knowledge controlled by the settler state. Compartmentalized
from their homelands, the individual is removed from
their sense of belonging (or un-belonging) and their place-
based responsibilities. Individualism is made possible by
the compartmentalization of our expansive bodies to the
physical individual.

The compartmentalization of body from the larger web
of creation also represents a crucial ontological shift that
allows the relations around us to become objects. When the
body is removed from its inherent relationality, this separation and distinction permits an othering of the elements of
creation around us. Our bodies that carry our homelands,
our ancestors, and the great beyond, the muskrat, the moon,
and the rushing water, become just a physical vessel, and
all those beautiful relationships become other and object.
When the body is not ancestor, ancestor can become
other—a distant abstraction of what should be our visceral
and agentive generational responsibility that extends to the
great beyond. When the body is not our homelands, the

land becomes object and resource, divorcing our sense of self from our inherent belonging to place. The ontological shift from expansive relationality to physical individual is fundamental to enforce our participation in the always violent existence of settler colonialism.

Beyond these fundamental compartmentalizations that generate the individual and define the world around us as non-relation and resource, the minutiae of colonial architecture are relentless with compartmentalization. Importantly, settler colonialism must not only remove us from our relationality but also hold us in place. We are most threatening to settler colonialism when we traverse its boxes and boundaries, swelling with the waters of our homelands to restore their sacred currents and flow. And so, the compartmentalization of life in settler colonial society is endless and insidious.

They do everything they can to keep us in place. And yet, we always spill over.

The spider builds many webs. While they work tirelessly to weave children to the great beyond, they also weave us toward a better future. The spider has always watched over us. They watched as settler colonialism descended like a black cloud on our relatives, and charted every step with their beautiful web. Over time, this web spanned the entire globe, marking the ways we are indubitably connected, cloaking the earth in silver threads made of stardust and hope.

The web of creation we are immersed within is expansive, spanning the metaphysical dimensions of our existence as well as the physical globe. Anishinaabeg have always been cognizant of our relationships to people across the world through the systems of trade and ceremony that brought us together. In the contemporary era, we are drawn into further global relationality by virtue of colonial empire and imperialism. Imperialism is the overarching structure that seeks to solidify colonialism by hegemonizing Western power as the unified front of empire. Imperialism, like a robust and rusty framework of violence, encases the globe in its clutches, binding and strengthening colonies through pathways of dispossession. Strongholds of empire such as the United Kingdom, the United States, and Canada rely on one another to bolster their power in order to solidify the structure of a global empire that protects and reinforces their individual domination. It is important to remember that our bodies here on Turtle Island grapple not only with settler colonialism but also with overarching structures of imperialism that implicate us in the global struggle for liberation.

The broader scaffolding of imperialism and Western hegemony relies on a grounding in compartmentalization that generates an individualism so deep that it stunts the way people relate to their own sense of responsibility and solidarity, even when orienting themselves toward justice and resistance. Through the compartmentalization of our vision of liberation to our local and experiential contexts, imperialism and settler colonialism further invisibilize themselves in order to ensure their persistence. There are many long-standing strategies for accomplishing this. Through the dehumanization of various racialized communities, we are encouraged to view the struggles of other oppressed peoples as separate from us through the lens of the other. Through the compartmentalization of our sense of self that removes us from the dimensions of global responsibility, we individualize our struggle and see external struggle as something too separate for us to participate in. Lastly, through the relentless violence of settler colonialism itself, many oppressed peoples do not have the capacity to learn about one another, show up for one another, and become invested in joint struggle because they are too busy surviving. These conditions are intentionally orchestrated by the settler state and imperial forces. They know that if we are able to truly understand the interconnections of our global struggle, then we will have the very real potential to dismantle imperialism and burn our settler colonies to the ground.

For much of my life, I focused intently on my specific experiences of settler colonialism in a localized and community-centred context. I dedicated my life to working with Native youth and providing them with anti-colonial education that might allow them to better understand and resist colonialism. Perhaps bolstered by the immense isolation of living and working in remote and rural Northwestern Ontario, I gave my full self to my community at the expense of any semblance of material solidarity with other oppressed groups. Solidarity was something I felt was important—for example, I believed Palestine should be free—but for most of my life I did not extend myself beyond these moral positionings. The urgency of my own community's survival overtook me, and for the entire decade of my twenties, I compartmentalized my own sense of liberation to be solely about my people.

But then the escalation of the genocide in Gaza in October 2023 changed me completely. Like cold water splashed on my face, so much of the invisibilized scaffolding of settler colonialism and imperialism began to crumble under the weight of this moment. I watched the footage of the genocide in real time and felt my ancestors standing at my side, lighting the fires of my responsibilities that extend to my global relations. I charted the codependencies of the settler colonies, understanding just how much Canada depends on the United States, depends on Israel, depends on the United Kingdom. I began to see the silver threads from the spider, who has worked so tirelessly to lead us into a future of wholeness for all our relations.

I cannot delineate exactly why it took me thirty years to materially orient myself around a free Palestine, but I can speculate that the compartments that settler colonialism makes are so invisible that it obscured the scope of my responsibilities, even as someone who was well versed in the effects of empire, colonialism, and power, and even as someone who was actively working for liberation. I state this here to demonstrate the enormity of what Palestine has taught many of us, what Palestine has woken up in Indigenous peoples across the globe—Palestine has succeeded in eroding some of the deepest infrastructure of empire, and this disintegration will continue to echo throughout this world and beyond. I also state my shortcomings here in order to normalize growth and expel ego from our movements for liberation, and to better understand pathways for the radicalization of our practices of joint struggle. This moment radicalized me, deeply and wholly, and spending time

understanding why and how helps me to encourage a deep-
ening of this process in both myself and those around me.

*I have been going to rallies for Palestine every single weekend.
I go not because I necessarily believe in the rally as a format
for change, but because it is the only place where anything
makes sense. A group of older Palestinian men, maybe the
same generation as my father, beckon me over and tell me they
are glad to finally meet the person who cares about Palestine
more than they do. We all laugh together. The deep familiarity of a very specific type of humour embraces us. They ask for
a photo and I am wearing my regalia. Normally, I might feel
hesitant—worried about being swallowed by the limitation
of my identity to this often fetishized representation—but
instead, I feel grace. There have been so many moments of
passing tension as our communities come together in this
critical moment, but they are all filled with such grace. The
settler state has never wanted us to truly see one another.*

In a practical sense, Anishinaabe liberation can never be
full without the liberation of all oppressed people. Palestine
taught me this, in my bones and in my body. We are too
enmeshed within the larger structures of empire to be able
to free our respective communities without also dismantling
the rusty and sharp framework of imperialism that encloses
us all. With the global visibility of the genocide in Palestine
and rising global outrage, imperial powers floundered to
maintain power and, in doing so, laid themselves bare. We
were able to witness the inner workings of imperialism in
broad daylight, with Israel, the United States, the United

Kingdom, and Canada working together tirelessly because one settler colony simply cannot exist without the others. This will be known as their greatest mistake—the radicalization of so many, through the witnessing of clumsy and blatant imperial function and force. On a practical level, we can now deeply understand that compartmentalized approaches to liberation will never be complete. This is not to say that community-oriented work is useless, but rather, that it must be done in conjunction with the global project of liberation, as a beautiful tending to one of the infinite silver threads that bind us together in wholeness and justice, a nod of deep reverence to the spider who weaves us all together.

In a spiritual and moral sense, Anishinaabe liberation must be attentive to our expansive web of creation that includes our relatives in Palestine, Congo, Sudan, Haiti, and beyond. Our responsibilities as Anishinaabe people have always traversed the expansive universe, but the urgency and overwhelm of colonial violence on our bodies and lands over generations has slowly compartmentalized our sense of responsibility to exclude our global human relations. Our responsibilities as Anishinaabe people cannot be compartmentalized to a web of creation that is limited by the settler colonial imagination. My ancestors told me so when they wailed beside me while I watched videos on my phone of displaced families being carpet bombed. My homelands told me so when they welcomed my Palestinian kin to our homelands in Treaty 3 territory with a loud crack of thunder and all the animals of the land coming to greet them. The spirits told me so when they helped me dream up a future of bound Anishinaabeg and Palestinian wholeness. It is precisely my

Anishinaabe identity, my wild and flickering body and the sacred smoke inside of me, that insists on an expansion of liberatory practice.

Understanding settler colonial compartmentalization teaches us how to evade it, and ultimately how to return to our wholeness and liberated states of being. As an Anishinaabe person, I refuse the compartmentalizations that attempt to render my body separate from my ancestors, my homelands, and all that I am and will be. As an Anishinaabe person, I refuse the compartmentalizations of my sense of liberation and justice that attempt to prevent my whole-body investment in global struggles against colonialism and imperialism. As an Anishinaabe person, I refuse the compartmentalizations of my child from the children of Palestine that attempt to keep me locked in an individualized notion of responsibility.

I spill over it all, with ferocity and without pause. I am everything they can never control. I am everything they can never touch. I am everything they can never be. My body, like smoke, travels to Palestine to bear embodied witness. My body, like stardust, flickers with the light of so many ancestors. My body, like water, seeps into every border, every dam, every crack in the imperial framework in order to one day obliterate it. Our greatest tool is the innate ability of our bodies to evade the compartmentalizations they so desperately seek to maintain.

The smoke inside of us can never be quelled.

In the eyes of our children, we can see the great beyond—swirling galaxies and the low moan of creation in their ancient gaze. In their eyes is also the deep knowing, a look of such profound seriousness for someone only days old. Our children travel with the knowledge of what kind of world they are entering. Indeed, it is how they prepare their gifts. They choose their life, despite the violence and the harm. In their gaze is the medicine for the futures we so desperately need. My daughter taught me this. The children of Palestine taught me this.

When we leave the place before birth, we climb onto the delicate spider's thread that leads us to the earth below, spiralling toward the earth like a leaf in the wind. We descend through the birth canal to meet our new physicalities and the gentle containment of the human experience that now belongs to us. Grief, love, hope, and pain are now ours to carry, held temporarily by the confines of linear time and space, only to be dissolved one day into the sparkling mist of the universe. Born to parents whose bodies may be battered and bruised by the settler colonial world, we open our eyes to greet them. Born to homelands flooded and bombed, cut open, and destroyed, we extend our arms to cradle them. Despite the harsh and violent world that awaits, we still carry inside our bodies the swirling smoke that whispers to us visions of a sweet and just future. And so, we choose to persist.

Chapter 3

The shape of my body

I have danced upon the spider's thread to descend from the stars. I am in my body now, and it feels like home. Instantly cradled by the new familiarity of the rise and fall of my breath, my soft belly swells with my fragile mortality. I am in my body now and it feels like unabashed joy. The feeling of euphoric impermanence as I take my first breath and howl with the tenacity of creation.

I was born on a snowy morning in January. During my mother's quick labour, I descended from the stars, travelling along the spider's thread to meet the narrow passageway that would squeeze me into existence. My mother was just twenty years old, but she speaks of my birth as an experience where she felt strong, connected, and unfaltering in her confidence to birth me whole. She was supported by my maternal grandmother, my father, and my two brothers. There is a picture of my young brother holding my tiny hand just after I was born with pure awe pouring from his eyes. I imagine myself in that moment—the pressure surrounding my new body as I contort and greet the blinding light of the hospital room, the feeling of spilling out yet being confined by a physical body outside of water for the first time, and then the warm embrace with my mother. I imagine what surrounded me in that moment—all my ancestors ushering me into this world with the same pure awe pouring from their eyes, the spider intently watching over us all, and the air thick with the vibration of creation.

My birth was a moment of wholeness for both me and my mother. I wish that I could write about how whole my body continued to be as I grew from a baby into a woman, but my body was also born into the settler colonial world.

When I was born, my homelands and stardust came with me. When I was born, my ancestors sang a song of celestial joy and justice. When I was born, my spirit helpers ruptured the great beyond to deliver me into breath. But my ancestors also knew they had to whisper strength into my ear, and the spirits held me in one last embrace before the storm.

Here on earth, my homelands shift, moan, and move with the pulse of the universe. Anishinaabe bodies flicker under the moonlight, and then disappear into the night sky with a flash of iridescent light. My ancestors are so tangible they are almost visible—past, present, and future contained within a moment of running my hands through the dewy grass. If all was right with the world, I would have been born into this spectrum of creation, unabated and undisturbed.

My body, whole and full, would enter the stream of creation like a drop of sacred water running through my homelands. My body, whole and full, would spill out of my mother's to meet the river that surrounds us. My body,

whole and full, would be adorned with the inherent movement of creation, hair reaching stars and galaxies swirling in
my palms. But in the settler colonial world, the movement of
creation is not permitted. We are born into rivers dammed,
our bodies brushing up against the cold concrete borders
of colonialism.

The inherent and unrestrained movement of creation has
always posed an existential threat to the rigid requirements
of structural oppression. By necessity, settler colonialism is
a project of attempted stillness so that it may contain and
control the wild pulse of exuberant creation. Boxes, boundaries, and harsh lines cut across body and land, attempting to
hold us in place. In the broadest sense, they cut the land up
into parcel and piece through rail and road. They removed
the density of creation through logging and mining. They
blocked the water until we felt like we were going to burst.
With the Indian Act, they forced us onto small parcels of
land called reserves. With residential schools, they removed
children from their families. They outlawed our ceremonies
and prevented us from gathering. They worked so hard to
quell the movement of creation.

Settler colonialism can only enforce this stillness with a
violence so unnatural that it echoes throughout the universe
as an anomaly. A violence that, at times, feels otherworldly
in its utter terror. A violence that erodes, contorts, and
compresses Anishinaabe bodies and homelands. Our bodies
and lands are marked by this violence—made smaller, made
stiller, parts of us giving out because of the sheer force
around us.

Rather than being born into a stream of swirling creation,

my body left the waters of my mother to be held still by the compression of boxes and compartments surrounding the curvature of my physical form. I look to my parents and I cannot see complete wholeness. I look to my grandparents and I cannot see complete wholeness. All around me, I see a world where we must struggle to glimpse the wholeness that is our inherent right and work tirelessly to breathe life into the movement of creation.

My father wanted us to carve a black ash tree together, in the old way. First, we would find a tree struck by lightning. Then, we would dig it out of the earth with our bare hands, no matter how long it took. At night, we would sleep in the bush, lining up our beautiful bodies with specific constellations so that we could dream the carving designs. When he told me this, I saw my great-grandpa Pete. I saw my father as a little boy, standing by his side as they traversed our glorious homelands.

Before I can talk about my own body's topography, I need to talk about the bodies of those I come from, both people and place. This exploration of who I am constitutes an extended self-location, marking both the heart of, and limits to, my knowledge in relationship to the content of this book. I start with my ancestors, but now I do so in reference to their solely earthbound forms. My paternal great-grandparents, Agnes Wayash and Pete Kabatay, were fierce Anishinaabeg who kept the fires of our resistance lit, ensuring our collective survival amid the settler colonial storm. Their spirits are kept alive in my family through the stories we share and the ways we remain connected to them through our bodies. I feel particularly connected to my great-grandpa Pete because we share the same helper of the bear. The bear medicine in my life has always been an overwhelming presence that binds me to my responsibilities that extend to me from the great beyond. I am lucky to not only glimpse my great-grandparents through my father, who was raised by them deep in the bush, but also to feel their love, care, and guidance in my own body.

When my father was an infant, his father, Lawrence, drowned at Lac des Mille Lacs. The death of my grandfather marked a disconnect from my father's paternal side. My father was raised with the help of his maternal grandparents and spent most of his childhood living out our old ways within the expansive flow of our homelands. During this time, settler colonialism was reaching its rigid limbs into Northwestern Ontario with more force, but there were still lots of places deep in the bush to escape to. My dad speaks of our ancestral home sites spanning from just west of Thunder Bay, over to Winnipeg, and down into Minnesota before the border with the United States was solidified. He can point out places he has lived in Quetico Provincial Park and on the Seine River. He speaks of the years living with his grandparents as some of the greatest times in his life, when he got to hear our old stories told sprightly by the mouths of his brilliant and fearless grandparents.

My paternal grandmother, Agnes Kabatay, shows the same adoration for *her* parents by embodying their knowledge and gifts in her own life. My father, my late auntie Norma, my siblings, and I are all members of Lac des Mille

Lacs First Nation. However, my grandmother's other children are members of Couchiching First Nation, and my grandmother currently belongs to Mitaanjigamiing. My grandmother's parents were from Seine River reserve, whereas my father's paternal side were from Lac des Mille Lacs. All these reserves are in Treaty 3 territory, and traditionally our people moved freely across our larger land base. Although my father has thought about switching bands to be on the Seine River reserve, we remain with Lac des Mille Lacs to ensure that we preserve our presence within a land base that has been hit particularly hard by forced displacement and dispossession. The reserve designations in my family are relatively arbitrary, which is a reflection of how our people were mobile, flowing wildly with creation. The most important locator that we maintain is our relationship and belonging to Treaty 3.

Around the time Treaty 3 was signed in 1873, the people who were living in the region of Nezaadiikaang, or what is now known as Lac des Mille Lacs reserve, were known to be some of the most political and strong-willed in the region. We did not want to sign the treaty and were proving to be a continual thorn in the side of the early colonists who wanted to formally settle the region. Settler colonialism is cunning and strategic, responding most violently to its largest threats. Intentionally, the government chose to construct a series of hydroelectric dams on our reserve land that would flood not only our traditional territory but also the reserve itself, making our homelands unlivable for generations. Stated differently, the government first forced Anishinaabeg of that region onto a tiny parcel of our homelands and soon after forcefully expelled us from even that tiny parcel of land. These hydroelectricity projects would power the province of Ontario while our homelands became artificially submerged beneath the settler colonial swell.

The land must have been so lonely when we all left. The animals and spirits, frogs and spiders must have mourned us under the stillness of the moon. The muskrat, trying to build its new world, would be destroyed again and again with the rise and fall of the dam. The fish, slowly filling up with mercury, were helpless to protect their young from its impact.

When I was a baby, my mom and dad travelled to Lac des Mille Lacs with a group of our family to protest our inability to reside there. Their intention was to construct cabins from the land, demonstrating our sovereignty and tenacity to enact what is our inherent right. I was all cheeks, swaddled in green mesh, while my grandma and all the elderly women taught the younger men how to use chainsaws. They built cabins while I sucked on my toes in the sweltering summer heat, but they had to abandon the project when some men arrived with shotguns. Settler colonialism is so cunning and intricate; once it removes the Indigenous people from the land, there are so many invisibilized and overt mechanisms that cement its power.

The muskrat cries for the sun. Beside their family's home, in ruins, they weep for the sun to dry up the earth and for their home to persist. They follow the shoreline instinctively when they are ready to build their homes. And without notice, the water rises because of the dam and submerges them completely. The shoreline takes the hit. The shoreline is eroded and changed by the ebb and flow of an unnatural tide. Many beings weep at this change. Anishinaabeg cry for the sun. Beside their ancestral homelands, they weep for the sun to dry up the earth and for their homes to persist. But without notice, the settler colonial tides submerge them completely so that they must try once again to build their homes.

This hydroelectric project in our territory prevented Anishinaabeg from accessing their reserve for generations. We went from being some of the most politically steadfast people to being unable to even exist in a community beside one another. This was wholly intentional, the result of government action undertaken with the goal of subduing our rising resistance. Although reserve designations can be relatively arbitrary within the region, they unfortunately define our limited rights afforded through the Indian Act to necessities such as housing and livelihood. Being unable to live on our reserve effectively pushed many people to seek refuge and survival in urban centres, and many community members ended up living in many different places. Today, the reserve reflects this lived reality of disconnection through displacement. And so my dad remains a member of Lac des Mille Lacs instead of switching bands—in order to assert his presence as someone who grew up on our homelands and can trace his lineage to the Treaty 3 region for generations upon generations.

After seven years of living in the bush with my great-grandparents and migrating cyclically throughout Treaty 3 territory, canoeing and walking as their main modes of transportation, immersed in our old ways, my dad and Auntie Norma were forced to attend residential school. They attended St. Margaret's residential school in Fort Frances, Ontario, which was nothing short of a horror story, a genocidal attempt to completely destroy Anishinaabe spirit and body. At the school on the shore of Rainy Lake, Anishinaabe children were brutalized, tortured, and killed in incomprehensible ways—a violence so unnatural it echoes throughout the universe. When my father got out as a teenager, he could not live on our reserve because of the flooding from the dam. He also found it too alienating and painful to live with family members in Treaty 3 because of everything he had just endured. Residential schools were a silent explosion— children bore the brunt of the violence, but every single person in a community was affected in complex ways. My father left our homelands and began frequenting urban centres such as Toronto and New York, where he became an artist.

The impact of residential school in Treaty 3 territory is immense, but in our region it largely only directly affected one generation. Importantly, this is not a shared experience in many other regions where multiple generations of residential school survivors suffered sustained imposition. My father and auntie were the only generation to attend residential school in my family. In my grandmother's generation, they experienced the day school system, which was similar to residential school in its genocidal intent, but ultimately less isolating because children would return to their families each day. They also experienced the sanatorium system, which removed Anishinaabe people from their homelands for little to no reason and tormented, abused, murdered, and medically experimented on them. My grandmother's sister was taken to the local sanatorium, but my grandmother "only" had to attend day school.

My father's displacement from our territory is multi-dimensional and reflects a shared experience with many people of this generation from Treaty 3 who attended residential school. They survived not only the attempted genocide of the residential school system but also the subsequent alienation and complex trauma coupled with layers of forced displacement as a result of resource extraction. In Treaty 3, settler colonialism stole people's ability to have a home on their homelands, then on their reserve, and then with their families. Finally, settler colonialism stole people's ability to find home within their own bodies.

My father always has to be moving. As a young man, he could be found on specific street corners in Toronto, laughing away with my uncle Steve, selling artwork for cash. A whole generation had to find a sense of home on the streets. The layers of colonial violence that affect my father tell me that our existence as full and whole beings is deeply threatening to the forces of settler colonialism. They knew that if they did only one of these atrocious things to us, we would persist. In their fear and weakness, they gave it everything they possibly could, all at once.

And we still persist.

I dropped my dad off at the Nipigon gas station on a frigid January winter's day. It was time for him to start moving again. He looked at me with a huge smile and told me not to worry. He told me that people always pick him up, and that if they don't, he has a solar blanket and knows how to stay warm in a tree well. He could see the worry on my face. He told me that being cold brings us closer to our spirit and reminds us of our fleeting humanity; that it is a beautiful thing to feel that fragility, and that is part of our way. He didn't freeze to death when a Thunder Bay cop dropped him off far from town on a freezing winter night. He didn't freeze to death when he ran away from residential school, navigating through the bush to find home. He will stay warm as he hitchhikes from Thunder Bay back down to Toronto, walking the endless highway he has travelled so many times before.

My dad became a wandering artist who loved the big city and found community in other Native people of his generation who were also displaced to urban centres. He sold his artwork on street corners but also did exhibitions in galleries, flickering between worlds.

At this time, my mother was engaged in activism and solidarity work, largely informed by her parents' participation in the fight for Indigenous rights of the 1970s to '90s. My maternal grandparents were Scottish and Irish immigrants who moved to Canada in their twenties. My grandmother Peggy worked as a bank teller and my grandfather Harry was a plumber. They aligned themselves with the struggles of Indigenous peoples at the time, though this does not negate their complicity in settler colonialism. Despite aligning themselves with Indigenous sovereignty, my grandparents and mother still participated in and benefited from settler colonialism. In order to truly sabotage their settler identities, they would have had to remain in constant examination of their privileges and sense of responsibility, a messy and incomplete process for them. I wish with all my heart that my grandmother could have lived longer so that I could sit at her kitchen table and explore these nuances with her.

My grandmother Peggy was a special person, a fiery Irish woman with piercing blue eyes who wouldn't take crap from anyone. She was also deeply community-oriented and knew every single person on our block of St. Clair intimately. She passed away when I was fifteen, and at her funeral an endless line of people we had never seen before told us how Peggy had changed their lives.

My grandmother talked about Palestine at our kitchen table. My grandmother punched a cop in the face for racially harassing a Black man on her block. My grandmother would call me away from cartoons to smudge at the kitchen stove. My grandmother and I would regularly sing and get our feet washed at the Santeria church down the street, and afterward, she would visit with the women there for hours. My grandmother housed and hid a woman from the American Indian Movement in her tiny apartment. She was a part of so many communities in accountable and non-extractive ways, not because she thought it was what she should do but because these were the people who were a part of her world. She wanted a better world. She was my world, and her death rocked me.

My grandfather Harry was a stubborn Scottish man robust as rock. Peggy was the love of his life, and I think he mostly just tried to keep up with her. He also grappled with alcoholism and struggled most of his life to give and receive love. Yet as it often goes with grandparents, he was somehow able to love me fully and wholly. He showed his adoration for me in our endless park runs, his enthusiasm for my culture, and his consistency as a caregiver in my life. My grandpa always had a huge Canadian flag with Sitting Bull covering the maple leaf hanging in his room. He loved my dad and brothers, and connected with them through his disdain for English colonists and what they did to the Scottish people. Some of my fondest memories of him include running out in a Toronto rainstorm together and lying in the gutter to let the rushing water cover us completely, him walking me up and down the hall at my grandma's apartment while I cried myself to sleep on his shoulder, and his utter joy while he played Black Sabbath for me and insisted we turn off all the lights so we could be immersed in the music. I don't think anyone has ever loved me more than my grandpa.

I loved my grandparents deeply, and they played a big part in raising me. My mother worked long shifts, but we lived across the street from my grandma and I would spend many nights over at her place. My grandparents embraced my father and my brothers, who had a different mother from me. But they had struggled as parents, and my mother bore the brunt of their dysfunction. She carried the brutal weight of my grandpa's alcoholism, which she had experienced since she was a young child. At a very young age, my mother had experienced multiple instances of life-shattering violence that would never be addressed with her parents. At just eleven years old, my mother was sleeping alone in stairwells. At nineteen years old, she became pregnant with me. She has always told me that I saved her life; that without me, she is certain she would not be here anymore.

During the Oka Crisis in 1990, my grandparents camped out at Queen's Park in Toronto. They were very invested in this struggle, and my grandpa even sent his big white plumbing van to be used on the front lines. My mother was also involved and ended up at Oka. My parents met at a solidarity rally for Oka. My father was a tall and cool artist with his signature braided hair and bandana, and my mother was a young and beautiful nomad with a twist of punk creativity. Soon after, I was born—an Oka baby, birthed from a very complicated solidarity but from some semblance of resistance, nonetheless. My mom and dad raised me together for a couple of years before my dad had to start moving again. Despite the hardships of transitioning to the role of single mother, my mom has always told me that those early years were pure bliss for her and marked the first time she felt rooted in her body.

My mother is one of the most resilient people I know. Born into a web of chaos, she is the true definition of a survivor in no uncertain terms. She raised me as a single mom, with my dad as an ebbing and flowing presence in my life, and with her own parents as solid caregivers for me but whose care didn't necessarily extend to her in the ways that she needed. During my early life, she grappled with intense PTSD and undiagnosed manic depression, while still being a young person herself and trying to raise a baby. She has always had an open-door policy for my father, meaning no matter how angry she might have been, or how much I might get hurt, he was allowed to pick me up whenever he wanted. She has always done her best to foster my connection to my culture, forming strong relationships with my brothers' mother, who is also from Treaty 3, and with urban Native folks in the Toronto area so that I could have Native community around me as a child. I have fond memories of taking Anishinaabemowin classes with my mom at the Native centre in Toronto and attending ceremony at Wikwemikong. As a single mom now myself, I have so much respect and esteem for my mother's tenacity.

My father, whose nickname in Treaty 3 is "Leaf," blows like the wind across the land. It wasn't until I was an adult that I fully understood the origins of his way of being and why he always has to be on the move. He is also a survivor, in no uncertain terms. Despite the barriers he faced to parenting his children in fullness as a result of residential school and colonial violence, he has never faltered in instilling our Anishinaabe way of being into me. When I was a little girl, he would show up on our doorstep and carry me on his shoulders across town to sell his artwork, and I would witness an alternative relationship to creative practice. He would tell me the stories of his grandparents and that we come from the stars. He would push me in shopping carts across the hot city to go to late-night movies while he shared what he has endured in his body. Most of all, he simply embodied our worldview with ferocity and absolution. He didn't have to teach me how to be Anishinaabe; he showed me that we live it.

Everything is a swirling spectrum on the land. The soft trickle of water over rock creates the riverbed in the creases of my

palms. The distant murmur of frogs and bugs as unassuming
as the rise and fall of my own breath. Creation is always
overflowing, bubbling up, frothing at the mouth of the great
beyond.

My body was born from my weeping homelands and
the bruised bodies of my mother and father—an imper-
fect origin story of inherited grief, compressed bodies,
and razor-sharp violence around me in the people I loved
most. The first compression of my body happened when I
began to understand what my parents had endured in their
own bodies, my child mind trying to conceive of what kind
of world could possibly produce these harms. I became
conscious in a new body, just to begin to feel the loss of
wholeness in those around me, a dull and heavy weight
pressing on me. As a child, I used to fantasize about what
true happiness could look like, not for myself but for those
close to me. I would daydream about taking my grandpa on
a vacation and watching joy pour out of him that I had never
seen before. I returned, over and over again, to a memory
of my mother truly laughing and what her face looked like
wrinkled with contentment. Even as a child, I was learning
to orient myself toward the pursuit of a wholeness I could
not always see in those around me. The compression of my
body and the flattening of my form, relentless.

I was forced to grow up fast and be self-reliant, a lonely
kind of introduction to the world but one that I don't fault
anyone for. Since I was a child, I have had my own life in
order, creating for myself the stability I needed. I retreated
into my own experience, using art to explore the swirling

smoke inside my body that I could always feel despite the hardships. My identity as an Anishinaabe person was so certain and unfaltering, I never had to find myself; it was all just pouring out of me from the minute I was born. The certainty of my identity, and my rootedness in my Anishinaabe worldview, made the juxtaposition with my lived experience loud and lonely. As a young person growing up in the urban core of Toronto, I mourned the distance between myself and my homelands viscerally, yearning for the swirling smoke inside me to permeate the birch stands that I come from. As a young person, I mourned the distance between myself and my family, lighting the fire of my pursuit for wholeness for us all. Painting and writing became my sovereign space for splashing my knowledge, ancestors, homelands, blood, and tears into beautiful colour.

As I grew, I was shielded from a lot of colonial violence by my proximity to whiteness through my mother and maternal grandparents. I never had to worry about being taken away from my mother. I never had to worry about getting proper medical care because my white mom would be sitting beside me. My grandma would forget to pick me up from school for hours, but the secretaries would never question my care. The profound privilege of whiteness does not apply only to those who are white-passing but also to one's proximity to whiteness. Although I am racialized, my younger experiences are predominantly protected within the bubble of privilege from my caregivers. I hold these experiences alongside those I have witnessed in my Anishinaabe family members who do not have any proximity to whiteness—visiting my baby brother in a foster home, watching my brothers grapple with overt racialized violence, and feeling the clear difference in how my siblings and I are treated without the presence of my white family. As I became an adult and transitioned into a life where my basic necessities were not mediated by whiteness, I began to face more direct forms of racism. But still, the privilege afforded by my proximity to whiteness persists in the ways I am versed in advocating for myself and navigating a system that benefits whiteness.

My proximity to whiteness has shielded me from many forms of harm that my Anishinaabe family and community grapple with, yet settler colonialism is immersive and pervasive, and has reached me in other ways. I primarily experience direct settler colonial violence through my body and its non-consensual encounters. These experiences jolt my body, knocking off pieces of me to reveal empty holes that wind pierces through, the feeling of always being cold and hollow. My first non-consensual experience happened before my first moon and before I understood what puberty was. My little brown body was trespassed at a time when I didn't even understand what sex or romantic love was. I remember being frozen in shock, and afterward, all I could do was look at myself in the mirror for what felt like hours. Even at such a young age, shame is a tool made readily available to us by a settler colonial world that relies on certain bodies being seen as disposable and violable. My small and developing mind tried to soothe my writhing body by offering an explanation I still grapple with to this day—*This is how it is supposed to be.* Little Quill took a deep breath while looking in the mirror and found the only comfort in telling herself, *It is okay. This is how it is supposed to be.*

I think about my homelands holding me. Did they weep for me? Did they wail? I imagine them holding my small body with the soft moss of spruce bog, the roots beneath me cradling the shape of my body. They move earth and rock to create a place for me to land. It was in this moment that I first realized I could take a step away from my own body. My homelands witnessed me in this moment and began to sing a song that would one day, eventually, call me back. It would take decades. Will I ever weep for me? Will I ever wail?

This experience marked a sharp shift in how I related to my body. As I grew older and went through puberty, my experience as a Native girl would be characterized by a hypersexualization so immersive that I learned to stop looking people in the eye in public for fear of what I might witness in their gaze. It became easier to internalize my body as an object rather than acknowledge the violence, discomfort, and rage that lay underneath my experience. My ability to rationalize my own molestation can be attributed to the rampant dehumanization of Indigenous girls and women within the settler colonial world. Even as a young person, I had subconsciously internalized the idea that Native women were inferior, licentious, and for the taking.

Following the first breach of my body, I experienced more instances of non-consent where I needed to lean on the explanation that this is how it is supposed to be. Rather than chronicle my experiences of sexual assault, which were at the hands of both partners and non-partners, I presence them here generally as a central tactic of settler colonialism and a major contributing factor to my own disembodiment.

Importantly, all of my experiences of sexual violence were at the hands of white men and boys, and many of these experiences were characterized by overt connections to my identity as an Indigenous woman. In some instances, the intent to conquer and violate my body as an Indigenous woman was said out loud. There was nothing my body could do except harden into stone such that it might protect me. Each experience of non-consent is like a blow to this stone, parts of me falling off and cracks forming that I continually rupture out of like blood oozing from a wound.

I lived in Toronto until I was twelve and then moved to the small town of Fergus, Ontario, because my mother had a new partner and they were going to have a baby, my sister Nylah. My life changed fast and hard, and my discontent was visible through my dyed hair, black eyeliner, and experimentation with drugs and an exploratory lifestyle. Fergus is the Scottish capital of Canada—a mostly white, small-minded, and conservative town an hour and a half from Toronto where I stuck out like a sore thumb. The othering I experienced bordered on comical, even for a young person not yet versed in how to identify and articulate various forms of racism. On the one hand, I experienced continuous and sustained erasure in the incredulity that an Indigenous person could even exist, and on the other hand, I was called slurs like "wagon burner" and told to go back to my own country. These aggressions didn't faze me, but the more insidious and overwhelming fetishization of my body as a Native woman did. My entire high school experience was characterized by the hypersexualization and objectification of my body because I was visibly Native, and because I had already rationalized my first assault with the sentiment *This is how it is supposed to be*, I found myself living out that dynamic over and over again.

But even during my time of peak chaos in high school, I always had it together. When I was using hard drugs, even at school, I was still a straight-A student, a true testament to how deeply ingrained my hyper-independence was in my body. I got so much satisfaction from proving teachers wrong who would doubt my intelligence because I was Native, and even more so when I could do it while in a wildly altered state. Despite how isolated I felt, not just as a Native person specifically but even as a racialized person more generally in that homogenous setting, I did my best to carve out space for my identity. In grade ten I brought my dad in to speak about his experience in residential school after I was alarmed by how the subject was broached in my history class. I founded the Indigenous club, which was just me and one enthusiastic white teacher, but I had to try. By the end of high school, I had calmed down and was focused on getting out of Fergus and going as far away as I possibly could, which ended up being Vancouver, British Columbia.

By the time I was in my early twenties, I was becoming resourced enough by friends and community to finally confront my experiences of non-consent. I had made some of my most important friendships and was surrounded by strong Native women whom I consider my kin to this day. Together, we went through a collective radicalization, learning about our experiences of settler colonialism through specific language and tools at university that allowed us to better strategize our resistance. I fell so deeply in love with the women around me—not least my three best friends Salia Joseph, Keisha Charnley, and Taylor Wale, who still stand beside me today, and I felt so honoured to be building a world alongside them.

Around this time, I also began to confront my internalized dehumanization that had led me to pursue a degree in biology when I had hurriedly escaped Fergus. I realized I had done so to prove my value in the context of feeling continually worthless to others, particularly those teachers and parents of friends who had questioned my humanity based on my Indigeneity. I decided to leap into what I really wanted to do—work with my own people through art on our own terms. I turned away from the sciences, and decided to move to Thunder Bay, a place that represented returning home to me.

There are many complex ruptures within my family that made my decision to move to Thunder Bay complex. At this time, I was not close with my paternal grandmother, but I wanted to be and made that a priority. Moving to Thunder Bay also meant seeing some paternal family members less due to the ways that they avoid coming home. Regardless of these complexities, I anticipated the move to be revolutionary for me, a moment I had been working toward my whole life, one where I could finally feel the swirling smoke inside my body convene with my homelands in the here and now. This move was also supposed to be the last move of my life, an anchoring and commitment to my responsibilities to my homelands and community.

I was lucky to find a small house on the shore of Lake Superior, Gitchee Gumee, where I would fall asleep to the sound of the waves crashing on the shore. The land there was so humbling, and I watched in awe as the seasons passed over my tiny house on the lake—the thunderbirds shaking the earth in the humid summers, the stillness of the water in the fall on a crisp morning, the guttural moaning of the ice on the frozen lake, the bears waking in the spring. I lived in that house for five glorious years. It is where I began to paint with more regularity and ferocity, and where I had the courage to look towards my own body and its experiences of non-consent in order to begin to transcend them. It is where I learned how to bead alongside my grandmother and aunties. I would harvest medicines in the small patch of bush on my road. It is where I would one night dream of a child taking me up into the stars, waking up on a cold January morning to understand without a doubt that I was pregnant. It was also where I would eventually experience a terrifying break-in, spurring my abrupt move into town. It wasn't perfect, but there was so much goodness that came from that time.

My paternal grandmother, Agnes Kabatay, is a respected Elder in the Treaty 3 region. She is one of the strongest people I know, and in her eighties she still scales cliff faces to pick medicines for her family. We sit around her kitchen table beading for hours, listening to the stories of my grandmother's life that animate our ancestors and ways of being. Although many in my family struggle to show outward expressions of loud love, we know how to do so through action. My auntie Mary Lou helped me make my first jingle dress, and I got to dance beside them and my grandmother. My cousins Casha and Kaitlyn helped me raise my young daughter when I hurriedly moved to the city from my house on the lake. My auntie Norma would give me the earrings she made and always texted me when to put ash on my forehead. My grandmother cooked for us—scone dogs and wild rice like a warm blanket waiting for us across the ice road. My grandmother holds it all together, and she holds everyone together. She has been through unfathomable struggle, yet she still has so much to give.

Camping at Huronian Lake with my grandmother, auntie Mary Lou, and cousins Casha and Kaitlyn. My grandmother showed us where she used to live as a child, and we all slept under the stars while the spirits of the land rejoiced at our collective return. I struggled to make a fire with damp wood, and my grandmother basically snapped her fingers and a roaring fire appeared. We forgot to pack coffee and all got caffeine withdrawal headaches while my grandma chuckled to herself. We set a net and caught way too many fish. We practised our brutish Anishinaabemowin while my grandma laughed and shook her head. We gave the ancestors a good laugh.

I lived in Thunder Bay for seven years before I decided to leave, a gut-wrenching decision filled with complex grief. I had to walk away from my homelands, from our medicines, from the crisp and cold winters and endless summer days of Northwestern Ontario.

It was the city itself that burnt me right out. Thunder Bay is a place where settler colonialism is laid bare—the bodies of Native youth found in the waterways, human trafficking, anti-Indigenous violence, and police corruption. As someone who did work that actively challenged white supremacy and settler colonialism, I constantly felt physically unsafe. And I felt lonely within this work. Too few people around me wanted to challenge our conditions, and too many people around me wanted only to fight for inclusion. This is not to discredit the people of Thunder Bay—there are many amazing people I consider my dear friends and kin who are pushing boundaries, but there simply wasn't enough of us for me to feel truly supported and seen.

When my daughter was born, I stayed in Thunder Bay because I wanted to raise her on her homelands. But after nearly three years as a single parent, I realized I wasn't happy and needed the support of my mother and father.

I always had to be so diligent. We are always calculating risk and bracing for the tension of white supremacy encasing our bodies, holding them still in place. It felt like every time I spoke, I was confronting white fragility escalating into violence. It felt like every time I was perceived, I was confronting disgust. Yet these experiences were held by my glorious homelands. Being able to sit with my grandmother, being able to roam Treaty 3, being able to glimpse wholeness made it all worth it. One day I will return.

All of these experiences generate my body's topography. The shape of my body is uneven, eroded, and compressed by the weight of the settler colonial world. With each blow to my body, I am unable to retain my movement, unable to move wildly with the flow of creation. With each blow, settler colonialism keeps me more still, keeps my beautiful body from vibrating with the breath of my ancestors. My experience stands alongside the various experiences of my relatives who grapple with different and similar forms of overt settler colonial violence. The compression of our bodies comes from the weight of the settler colonial structures around us, the harsh scaffolding of settler colonial structures pressing down on our bodies to hold them in place. The erosion of our bodies comes from the relentless dehumanization of body and self that attempts to make us small. The breakage of our bodies comes from the direct violence that renders us into bits and pieces. It is all so relentless. We escape the compression, the harms, the erosion, and the losses by travelling far away from our beautiful bodies.

Chapter 4

I can't find my body in this cold night
Settler colonial disembodiment

The tightness of colonialism—that choking feeling in the back of my throat. I am unable to find home in my body, unable to find my body in the long and dark night. It happens when we are still so young, trying to understand the world around us. Our bodies become strangers to us.

Our bodies are the sacred homes of the human experience. We are supposed to land in them fully and wholly, delighting in our senses and marvelling at the sweet relationality our bodies lend us. When we run our fingers slowly over our skin, we may feel the wonders of the universe within us. When we sit quietly with ourselves, we may feel the dull hum of our ancestors' heartbeats and the electricity of their knowledge and love within us. When we walk, we may feel our homelands throbbing in our feet, frogs and muskrats spilling out with each step. But the violence of settler colonialism is immersive and permeates deep into bone and belly; its totalizing dimensions both suspend and pervade us.

Settler colonialism is, at its core, genocidal. Not only has settler colonialism oriented itself explicitly around the

genocide of Indigenous peoples in order to remove our
bodies from the land permanently, but it has also built its
societies around the enforcement of mass disembodiment.
Through hypercapitalism, we are robbed of our time and
subjected to a pace of life that supersedes connection with
both ourselves and others. We are enmeshed in a system
of value that prioritizes wealth and material success at the
expense of connection. In the latest frontier of neo-settler
colonialism, we wade through the dystopic sludge of techno-
fascism, clinging to our attention spans and capacities to
process information as we are encouraged to travel far away
from our bodies. Disembodiment is the act of retreating
from one's body, with the understanding of the body as
inseparable from our homelands, ancestors, relations, and
the great beyond.

Here on Turtle Island, where the physical architecture
of settler colonialism has been relatively solid for generations, the compartmentalizations of this world affect the
minute filaments of our relational webs—how we relate to
knowledge itself, how we relate to time, how we relate to
our sense of value, and how we relate to the rise of digital
technology that mediates our experiences. All these strategies directly support the material necessities of the settler
colonial project—the genocide and removal of Indigenous
bodies from our homelands, the manufactured consent and
inaction of those who witness and contribute, and, most
importantly, the insidious solidification of larger global
structures of empire and imperialism that strengthen localized settler colonies.

Settler colonialism is always attempting to remove

Indigenous bodies from their homelands in order to maintain the capitalist occupation and expansion at its core. There are layers to this process of removal that include removing Indigenous bodies entirely through death, physically removing us from our homelands through displacement, and removing the self from the body through assimilation and harm. All three of these methods of removal serve the original intent of colonialism. Although the removal of self from body does not constitute a straightforward process of clearing the land, it does impact our ability to be present in our bodies and to have the capacity to resist our dispossession. When we are less present in our bodies, we may have less capacity to fight for our homelands, to protect ourselves and our communities from harm, and to exert our energy to dismantle our settler colonial conditions. However, even in our most disembodied states, the presence of our homelands still hums within flesh, the warmth of our ancestors still cradles our bones, and the pulsing knowledge of the universe still flows through our veins. The inherent wholeness of our bodies has always deeply threatened the forces of settler colonialism, and so they continue to target the relationship between Indigenous self and body.

The night is cold yet muted. He knows he is freezing, but he can't feel the bite in the air. He floats beside a long highway, looking for cars that will give him a ride. He is going somewhere, but he doesn't care where. His form is tall yet hard to make out. The night is so cold, reaching minus thirty in the dead of winter in Northwestern Ontario, but he has to keep walking. He is always walking. He is like a leaf blowing in the wind. I dropped my father off at a gas station in Nipigon and watched him fade into the night.

The settler colonial removal of Indigenous self from body happens through two mechanisms. The first is assimilation, an attack on one's sense of self and identity through ontological impositions that do not recognize Indigenous identity or humanity. Assimilation coerces us through shame and violence to change the self and to only acknowledge the physical dimensions of the body. We grow further away from our body as a conduit of expansive relationality and deny the reality of who we truly are.

The second mechanism is direct harm to our bodies. In the settler colonial context, our bodies are battered and bruised, hated and harmed. When our bodies become saturated with harm, we retreat from the site of violence. We retreat from our bodies. The intended outcome of our disembodiment is that it becomes easier to control our bodies, easier to dispose of our bodies, and easier to clear our bodies from the land.

While sometimes this intended outcome is successful, sometimes it is not. Anishinaabe people have learned how to use disembodiment as a calculated strategy to survive the conditions of immense violence around us. We flicker between many states of presence in our bodies, the swirling smoke inside us calling us home and then letting us travel far away in the rhythmic tides of creation that pray for our persistence.

Disembodiment, the ability to take a breath and survive. Disembodiment, the feeling of losing your own body, the panic of not being able to find something so important when the night is growing dark. Disembodiment, the act of travelling so far from your own body so that you do not have to look at how it has been harmed. Disembodiment, turning away from realities of violence that are so incomprehensible that we cannot bear to look at them. Disembodiment, a cold and muted place to reside akin to not being able to find or feel your body in a dark and endless night.

The night is cold yet muted. I know I am freezing, but I can't feel the bite in the air. I float through a soft forest, hovering just above its cover. I am going somewhere, but I do not know where. I am not as calm as he was; I am panicked. It's like a bad dream to feel so formless, and I long for the comfort of home. The night is so cold, and I am looking for something. I cannot find my body in this cold night.

Disembodiment reverberates across generations. My own disembodiment began with my parents and how I absorbed the examples of their own disembodied states of being. It is interesting to inherit disembodiment from both my Anishinaabe father and my white mother, the violence they each experienced so immense yet incomparable. My father's disembodiment was heavily informed by residential school and myriad types of colonial violence. My mother's disembodiment was not related to race but to patriarchy, and she carried her own experiences of intense bodily violence that made it hard for her to be present in her body. As a young child, I was never shown what it looked like to exist fully in my body, and I came to understand disembodiment as a valuable coping strategy, while grappling with the grief of witnessing my parents existing in a muted state. As I got older, I learned more about the depths of harm my parents carry. Sometimes, we travel so far away from our bodies that the only thing left to do is to leave them completely. I imagine that my parents existed for a long time in that place deciding whether to stay or to go. For my mother, it was her pregnancy and my birth that kept her here.

Disembodiment, the act of travelling away from our bodies, is also a type of grief that can be inherited. Disembodiment, passed down through generations like lightning, renders us frozen in place with shock as we try to find our way back to our bodies in the endless night.

I wish to hold my parents when they were children in my loving arms. I wish to tell them that I love them and to whisper that they survived. I long to give them a gentle hug and feel the immediacy of their spirits within their bodies. I long to laugh with them, deep and guttural, in the hope that our laughter will carry them through what is to come. I wish to show them, as children, the chubby face of their granddaughter and the light of the pulsing universe that flows in her eyes. I wish to show them all the ways they shape a beautiful future.

Some wounds are so otherworldly in their violence that they reach the cosmic imprint of who we are in the great beyond. The generations emerging after these wounds are born with them and must work tirelessly to find their sovereign form. Residential school was one of these otherworldly assaults on the relationship between Anishinaabe self and body. Many children were killed outright and removed from the earth completely, a project of overt genocide. Many children took their own lives as teenagers and adults—the self travelling so far away from the body that it leaves completely. Those who remained, those who survived, could disembody themselves as a way to gain distance from the unimaginable violence they had endured.

Our disembodiment, however painful and unjust, has always been a valid strategy for our resistance. Our disembodiment, and our will to transcend it, can simultaneously be celebrated for the ways it has ensured our persistence.

Residential schools caused disembodiment through both strategies of assimilation and forms of harm that specifically targeted our relationships to our bodies. Anishinaabe children were taught that their bodies were dirty, worthless, and disposable, and they experienced the violent ontological imposition of a Christian worldview that didn't even recognize the Indigenous body as human. They were told that everything that makes them Anishinaabe, such as their bodies and beautiful brown skin, their ancestors, and their culture, was wrong. All the while, Anishinaabe children experienced sustained sexual abuse and torture, robbing so many of the ability to feel loved and worthy of wholeness in their bodies. They did everything they could to remove the self from the body. They knew that when we were planted firmly in our bodies, we were too powerful to contain, wild with the pulse of the universe, forever dancing with our ancestors, the water of our homelands rushing through our veins like swift rivers.

My father and late auntie Norma attended St. Margaret's residential school in Fort Frances, Ontario. Before they went to residential school, they roamed the vast and beautiful territory of Treaty 3 alongside their grandparents. I believe that this time spent living our old ways gave my father and auntie the resources they needed in order to persist through the horror they faced. When my dad got out of residential school, he could not live on our reserve, as it had been flooded by the government through hydroelectric dams. He became a drifting presence and began frequenting Toronto, New York, and the West Coast. He painted himself into the future, with vibrant colour and ferocious motion, using his creative practice to survive his experiences of sexual abuse, medical experimentation, torture, and horror that spanned nearly a decade starting at the age of seven.

St. Margaret's residential school was premised on brutalizing Anishinaabe bodies and spirits in ways that can only be characterized as evil and grotesque. I want to move us beyond the widely held understanding of residential schools as unfortunate and failed assimilation tactics operated by misinformed people toward the understanding that these schools were overtly and systemically genocidal. They mutilated, violated, and harmed Indigenous children relentlessly and with intention. The residential school system was not an unfortunate by-product of an aggressive assimilationist agenda—this *was* the project. The deranged violence perpetrated against the bodies of children was the project.

My father and auntie had to live through a horror story. Anishinaabe families in Treaty 3 had to live through a horror story. And as their children, we are left to make sense of an incomprehensible reality of violence. It is the incomprehensibility of this violence that invites us to disembody. The disembodiment of residential schools sought to rupture Anishinaabe spirits so violently from their bodies that the impact will undoubtedly be felt for generations, no matter how much individual work we do to heal in our lifetimes.

When you showed me where they cut you open, my own body ruptured and my guts spilled out onto the concrete between us. Blood soaking earth; guts cooking in hot sun—I tuck this moment deep into bone so I don't have to look at it. When you showed me where you tried to burn this place down, I silently got onto one knee and offered my back, ready to carry ten thousand Anishinaabeg out of this mess.

I feel the stories of my father's time in residential school in my bones. These stories must live in my bones because they are heavy and reach so deep. Even before the stories were shared, even at my birth, they were a dull weight that I learned to grow around and through. When I was born, my ancestors danced throughout my body with the joy of my existence. But they weren't done crying yet. As with their joy, I inherited their grief. And as I grew, I accumulated my own grief as I witnessed the dimensions of love that had been taken from me and my father. Hearing his stories for the first time felt like being gutted, followed by a dull and muted thud. The violence of that school was so incomprehensible that even hearing these stories was enough to cause me to disassociate and black out memories. My brain simply could not understand the realities I was learning about, so

I pushed so much of it deep into my bones. As I filled my bones with my father's stories, filled them up with our grief, my own grief, and my own experiences of violence and loss, I felt the weight of my skeleton become unbearable. I slowly retreated from my body so that I could feel some relief.

Father, your body is a bridge to the infinite, grounded in rock and sweat. Galaxies in your palms and stars in your heart, a thousand strands join you to creation. Father, you are life that persists, pushing me through the city in a shopping cart under a full moon. Line our bodies up with the constellations so that we may dream our art, put your pennies down.

The impacts of the residential school system continue to ripple throughout our families and across generations. Although much has been written about the tangible inter-generational impacts of these schools, such as the child welfare system, lateral violence, and addiction, less has been written about how these impacts manifest internally and how these realities land in the body. Residential schools specifically attacked the relationship between self and body in an attempt to clear the land of Anishinaabe children and communities. Through both assimilation and bodily harm largely characterized by grotesque sexual violence, they worked tirelessly to make our bodies unbearable, to make us hate our bodies, to render our bodies incapable of feeling pleasure and wholeness, to make us unable to give and receive the multi-faceted dimensions of love we deserve. Residential school survivors, against all odds, hold on to their bodies amid the stories of shame, guilt, pain, and confusion that now live in them. Many of us have travelled away from our bodies to escape the incomprehensible realities of violence that residential schools enacted on the people we love. Many of us have inherited a disembodied state from the survivors around us. Many of us have travelled away from our bodies because they do not receive the expressions of love we know we deserve in this life.

It is years later when my bones begin to ache—that moment again in the hot sun, guts leaking, as you told me how they operated on your tiny body and you still don't know why. Our grief is never just our own; it spills over bodies and land. We are always braced for the overflow, and it is my turn to burst.

Settler colonialism has always attempted to disrupt our capacity for love in order to clear the land and ensure its future. It has always attempted to disembody us to prevent us from accessing the expansive dimensions of love that make us Anishinaabe—the way the land adores us so, the feeling of never being truly alone, the lullabies of our ancestors recited into our babies' ears, the sound of a black hole, the ability to sacrifice our bodies in the here and now for the justice of creation. Our love was, and is, undefinable, boundless, and alive. Our love was, and is, a complex web of relations that far extends our own communities, traversing homelands, animal kin, and the spirits of the great beyond. Our love has always been the kind of love that holds our communities together, that weaves us into the fabric of our homelands, and that has always given us a purpose that extends far beyond our human experience. Our love has always been deeply threatening to the settler colonial project.

Through the residential school system they targeted the relationship between self and body not only as a mechanism of genocide and removal but also as a way to threaten our capacity to love. Each child removed from their family's arms was like a hammer falling onto stone, irrevocable cracks cascading across the land. They further distorted our understandings of love through the sexual violence and torture of children that ripples throughout generations. The impact of such horrific and sustained sexual violence on young children is complex. Some of the children who attended residential school grew up to become parents who could not express love, parents who enacted the same harms onto their own children, parents who were scared of their own identities, parents who were so disembodied that they walked away from all responsibilities, parents who could not bear to sit still.

When they cut your hair, they could not see the silk. When they cut your stomach, they could not reach the earth. When they raped your body, they could not be whole. When we rupture, our ancestors always dance around our wounds.

To be Anishinaabe and have a parent who attended residential school is to exist in complicated motion—on the one hand, I have mourned the expressions of love that have been stifled in my family, and on the other, I have marvelled at how our capacity to love shifts and evolves to pour out of us regardless of our disembodiment. When dreaming up our strategies for collective liberation alongside Palestinian kin, I joked that maybe they could teach us how to love again. As I said this out loud, a part of me wept silently. The truth is that I had been noticing how loudly Palestinian people love each other, how viscerally they love their homelands, and how unfalteringly visible they make their love for life. In particular, I had been noticing how fervently they love the children. Faces of Palestinian people wrinkling up into deep smiles at the sight of my three-year-old daughter at community events. Watching a man notice my daughter from across the room and hurriedly stuffing his pockets with candies; a moment later, she walked by him and he offered them to her with an exuberant expression.

On a trip with Palestinian organizers, I watched my daughter surrounded with complete and utter love, expressed unfalteringly and without pause as they played with her under restaurant tables and snuck her sweets at every pit stop. This wasn't the Anishinaabe love she was used to—at times expressed inconsistently, whispered through a shame that was never ours but that we can't quite escape, the eerie discontent of feeling distance in the people sitting right beside you. As intergenerational inheritors of residential school impact, we wade through the complexities of learning how to show our love after such nuanced, sustained, and unimaginable horror directly attacking our capacity to love. Palestine continues to teach me how to reclaim our love and how to once again love our children with ferocity.

Although dimensions of love in my family have been disrupted by the residential school system, it does not mean that the love is not there, but rather that it is hard to articulate and receive. Our love, whether or not it is expressed in its full dimensionality, is unwavering and ferocious. Our love traverses galaxies, and it will never be quelled by the violence of our earthside experiences.

Our love is what allowed my auntie to experience unthinkable harm yet remain such a caring and grounded person. She wrote her master's thesis on the concept of intergenerational trauma inflicted from residential school, one of the first voices to conceive of our trauma in this way. She returned to her body, against all odds, to open herself and understand her own pain as an act of profound love for her children, her family, and her community.

Our love is what allows my grandma to experience a lifetime of multi-faceted trauma yet remain a fierce carrier of our culture. After attending day school, losing multiple relatives to colonial violence, and having her children taken from her, she eventually became the glue that holds us all together, holding on to the old language, holding on to our old ceremonies, jingle-dress dancing us into a beautiful future.

Our love is what allows my dad to have his body broken, cut, abused, and tortured yet still be able to hold kindness and acceptance for all people. He persisted through his intended destruction to become a fearless man who demands a world of justice not just for our own people but for our Palestinian kin.

Can you see what they can never take from us?

Beautiful brown father, I am holding your tiny body under a blanket of stars. Playing with insects in the tall grass, you chuckle deep into your belly that has not yet been cut. In between gasps of laughter, I whisper that you are loved and beautiful and whole, spider silk dancing between past and future. Look at me, Father, I am whole and full. I am you.

Despite the horrors of residential school, my father has never faltered in making sure I know who I am as an Anishinaabe person. Despite the violence and the loss, he has painted colourful worlds that remind us of all that we are. Despite the assimilation, the cutting of his hair, the hunger experiments, the medical experiments, the torture, my father revels in the beauty of the universe and delights in the pleasure of what it means to be Anishinaabe. And although his body often dissolves, and he blows away like a leaf in the wind, he remains anchored in his own sacred ways to his children, his grandchildren, his homelands, and himself. It has always been the greatest honour to come from him. It will always be the greatest honour to be Anishinaabe and to come from such expansive love.

And so, I hold my auntie and father as small children. I give them a final hug and feel their spirits so close to their bodies. I whisper that they are so loved. And I send them both off into the still night, where they will encounter a vicious storm. And yet, loved in ways they can never touch. And yet, loved in ways they could never imagine.

I grew up knowing and understanding my parents' experiences of violence from a young age. Alongside my intergenerational entanglement with my parents' disembodiment, I accumulated my own experiences of bodily harm that made it hard to be present in my body. I have drawn upon disembodiment as the coping mechanism most readily available to me. The scale and scope of the violence my parents suffered warped my threshold for what is possible to endure in this world. For a large portion of my life, I discounted and minimized my own experiences of bodily harm because they were not as extreme as the horror of my father's experiences in residential school and my mother's experiences of multiple forms of sexual violence as a child and teenager. The world I was born into dictated the threshold for what we can and should endure, and so I buried a lot of my own experiences with this conception.

It is crucial to state again here the privilege I hold as a mixed person raised by my white mother. Her privilege covers me like an umbrella, shielding me from many forms of violence, while also extending opportunities I would not otherwise be afforded. I have never been beaten up in a public space for being Native. I have never been driven to the edge of town in the winter by the police. I have never been apprehended from my family. These are all experiences that my immediate family have had because they do not have the same proximity to whiteness that I do. Importantly, the scale of bodily harm we experience informs the impact that settler colonialism has on our relationship between self and body. My relative privilege allows me to experience a level of disembodiment that I am able to reflect upon and write about, and that I believe I am able to repair in my lifetime. Many of my family members and larger community might continue to exist in disembodied states for their own persistence.

Most of the harms my body has endured are tied to my identity as an Indigenous woman, and my proximity to whiteness has mostly restricted my experiences of direct bodily harm to the realm of sexual assault. I feel the weight of cisheteropatriarchy crushing my shoulders and spine, reverberating deep into my heart and belly. The weight is so immense because it is a central and long-standing structure of settler colonialism that has privileged cisgender, hetero-sexual men at the expense of others for generations. Since contact, the settler state has recognized how Indigenous women, Two-Spirit, trans, queer, and non-binary people are so deeply threatening to the colonial project, and as such, these people have always been the explicit target of the settler state.

The lived experiences of Indigenous women, Two-Spirit, trans, queer, and non-binary people cannot be homoge-nized, but it is worth stating that, collectively, these people bear the brunt of a specific form of settler violence intent on destroying our bodies. Since contact, our bodies have been deemed unworthy, disposable, and conquerable. Since contact, violence against our bodies has been state-sanctioned and encouraged as an effective tool to clear the land for settler occupation and expansion. They were so terrified of our power, of our ability to weave our commu-nities together, of our connection to the great beyond, that they targeted our bodies with ferocity. They could not comprehend the ways our bodies vibrated in the moonlight, the ways our pleasure reverberated throughout galaxies, the ways we made our communities unshakeable, and so they feared—and harmed—us deeply.

When we weep, the waters of our homelands softly comfort us as they travel across our skin. When we speak, our voices channel ancestors that they don't remember. When we dance, our bodies transform into smoke and swirl with the complexity of the universe. They have always harmed us for fear of what they will never have, what they could never even comprehend, what they can never reach. They have always wanted us to retreat far away from our bodies so that they can destroy them.

My interrogation of the power structure of cisheteropatriarchy is limited by virtue of my privilege as a cisgender person. I experience cisheteropatriarchy as someone who is both oppressed and privileged within this structure in different ways, and so there are nuances, and depths of violence, that are outside of my experience. Despite my experience being linked to my identity as a cisgender woman, it is important to emphasize that transphobia has been absolutely central to the settler colonial project, and that trans, non-binary, and gender non-conforming people have always been central to our communities and nationhood. It is also important to state outright that when I talk about the legacy of harm that Indigenous women face through settler colonialism, this implicitly includes all women. It is the settler colonial context that necessitates that I state this explicitly.

There are many examples of how the state has sanctioned violence against Indigenous women, including the pass system, the ongoing crisis of missing and murdered Indigenous women, girls, Two-Spirit, and trans people, forced sterilization, and the Indian Act, to name a few.

Although I will not dive into this legacy of harm, I will discuss the overlying binary that Indigenous women are forced to exist within. On the one side of this binary is the "good" Native woman who is an assimilated, polite, and docile Indian princess archetype. On the other side is the licentious, immoral, worthless, and dirty savage archetype. Importantly, on both sides of this binary, we are hyper-sexualized and rendered non-human.

This binary sustains the narratives that enable violence against our bodies. This binary also weighs heavily upon us and contributes deeply to our disembodiment. This binary props up the power structure of cisheteropatriarchy that is so integral to the settler colonial project. This binary is upheld through legislation and law, the representation of Indigenous women in popular culture and media, and the portrayal of our deaths and harms in courtrooms and to the public.

This binary is omnipresent and insidious in the colonial world. It continuously normalizes the dehumanization of Indigenous women and provides a justification for inflicting harm on our bodies. This binary has sustained generations of narratives that dictate the treatment of Indigenous women's bodies. This binary is one of the foundational mechanisms of settler colonialism that has always worked to remove the bodies of Indigenous women from the land. Indeed, I felt the effects of this binary from a very young age.

At the tender age of twelve I stopped making eye contact in public because of the stares from white men who looked like they wanted to harm and conquer me. When I was seventeen, a partner affectionately called me his "little savage." The hands of a partner just below my neck when I refused to have sex. The times I never said yes. The times I was told I was pretty for a Native girl. The times I have been called Pocahontas. I wish to travel back in time and sit with my twelve-year-old self to tell her she is human and exquisite, to hold her so close to my body that she does not take any distance from hers.

The binary imposed on Indigenous women serves an overarching narrative that portrays our bodies as conquerable and non-human. This narrative encourages and sanctions the genocide, violence, and violation that our bodies face in the settler colonial context. The violence we experience is twofold in that it occurs within our intimate lives as well as beyond our sphere of relationships. We can truly be harmed anywhere. My body was first violated when I was a child, an experience that put me into a disembodied state early in life. When I was a teenager, my body was violated and fetishized. As an adult, I have worked really hard to protect my body from violence, but I still carry the constant fear of being harmed outside my personal relationships. On top of my own experiences, I carry the stories of the ways my mother and other relatives experienced near-fatal violence on their bodies from strangers.

All these experiences normalized my own dehumanization and the lack of control I had over my own body. Especially as a child, when I was trying to make sense of my belonging and value in the world, I could not comprehend the ways my body was being mistreated by so many. I floated softly away from my body as a way to cope. I disembodied myself from presence within my own body, but also from the ability to feel pleasure and worthiness in my physical body. The bodily harms we experience as Indigenous girls and women are so relentless and dehumanizing that we often disembody ourselves just to be able to breathe.

I once begged the moon to make me feel. I couldn't find my body in the murky darkness. I once begged the moon to stay with me, whole, so that she could illuminate the dark night and I could find my body. At the edge of my skin, at the parts I don't like to touch, I feel the warmth of a fire not my own. Ancestors tending to my softness, always working to keep us whole. When I cry, it is a gift that brings me back to my body. The moon makes me weep with her as we look at all that has happened to this beautiful body of mine.

The violation of my body as a young person pushed me into a state of disembodiment that didn't allow me to be fully present in my body and that didn't allow me to take ownership over my own pleasure, desires, and wholeness. In my intimate life, I learned to be completely absent as a way to protect myself from the harms that I expected to happen. In my emotional life, I grew further away from my capacity to feel my emotions and existed as a stone wall. I was able to experience further harms and trauma without flinching because I wasn't fully present. I had become so skilled at my own compartmentalization and disembodiment.

Disembodiment, a muted relationship with my own body, is one of the central ways I experience settler colonialism.

In the hardest of times, I have felt like I cannot find my body within a long and dark night. In the easiest of times, I have still struggled to feel and process emotions in my body, living in an invisibilized loop of disassociation. However, the body itself is an agentive entity that has the capacity to love and care for us. Our ancestors call us back to our bodies when we cannot bear to look at them. We are always spilling over.

One day my body said, "Enough." At a time when I experienced true care and consent with a loving partner, my body ruptured and expelled all these experiences I had been hiding in my bones. Memories of my experiences of harm, and memories of my father telling me his stories of violence, came crashing out of me and lay on the floor for me to look at them. My body needed to shake me. My body was calling me back. This rupturing was incredibly painful and unsettling. I became uncomfortable with being touched at this time and was forced to reckon with my ability to black out painful experiences. This was the first time in my life that I had to acknowledge that I was living in a muted and dissociated state, and I started to think critically about the body as a site of colonial impact. This was also the first time in my life that I painted my own body. As my body ruptured, I painted myself feeling whole and good, full of pleasure, spilling over all my physical dimensions. I marvelled at this moment of wholeness that my body had given me.

In the soft veil of the weeping moon, the guardians of my softness wet my skin with blood and tears, and they pick blueberries from my perfect flesh. They soften my edges so that I may ebb and flow. They work my skin so it becomes tender, so that I may feel. I spoke with the moon and she made me whole.

Settler colonialism makes the night so dark and endless. It is persistent in its violence and cunning in its strategies to remove Indigenous bodies from our homelands. Settler colonialism is always attempting to remove the self from the body, as a way to distance us from the expansive relationality that is the foundation of who we are. The violence of the residential school system and the realities of bodily harm that Indigenous women face through cisheteropatriarchy are but two stories of many that spill onto our communities in complex ways. As Indigenous people, we are always experiencing multiple forms of violence that exist in complex and interlocking ways to inform settler colonial disembodiment. For this reason, disrupting our disembodiment is a non-linear process. We may do so much work to come back to our bodies, only to experience harm that pushes us into disembodiment again. We may flicker between various states of embodiment as we grapple with the ongoing forms of violence we face. But there is so much power in charting colonialism and understanding its strategies, because this also illuminates what is threatening to colonialism.

When it feels hard to be vulnerable about my own experiences, I think of my auntie Norma and the work she did after residential school to open herself up as an act of nurturing future generations of Anishinaabeg. When it feels hard to be vulnerable about my own experiences, I think of my mother and the ways she insisted on life for herself and for me by refusing to keep her stories hidden. When it feels hard to be vulnerable about my own experiences, I think of my father speaking truth to my tenth-grade history class, or the curious stranger asking about his art, or the crowd of people who gathered to fight for a free Palestine. Opening ourselves up is an act of expansive love that is informed by our responsibility to future generations. We often find the strength to open ourselves up, not through the love we have for ourselves, but through the love we have for those around us and our innate desire to help them feel whole.

When I open myself up, I swim back to my body and look at the stories it holds. When I open myself up, I flicker with my own embodiment, even if it is momentary, and even if it hurts. When I open myself up, I can finally find my body in the cold night. We will find our bodies in the dark and endless night.

INTERLUDE

A return to our swirling smoke

I am lying on the forest floor and I cannot breathe. Too many days of witnessing the genocide in Gaza, and today, I cannot hold my body up against the weight of this world. I press my forehead to the ground and let my tears speak to the land. The water that spills out of me is hot and salty, dripping onto the still-frozen ground beneath me. I have moved beyond crying— my face contorts into frozen agony as no sound escapes me except for my disgruntled breath. I don't recognize this part of myself. I cannot take it anymore. The dead children on my phone. The grandparents wailing in horror. Understanding, in an embodied way, what it feels like to live through this type of violence and what is to follow. I cannot take it anymore.

The smoke surrounds me in the forest.

The genocides of Indigenous peoples across the globe always target our beautiful children, the spirits who have so recently travelled to their bodies, who should be given the chance to delight in the complexity of existence. I imagine my grand-mother, whose children were stolen from her to be abused and tortured beyond what we ever could have predicted, now living through a time when Palestinian children are being murdered and harmed beyond the limits of human comprehension. Oh, the pain of it all. The pain of a single person who must experience, resist, and witness settler colonialism in all its ugly forms in a single lifetime. Oh, the children! Oh, the children! Oh, the children!

I am now lying flat on my back on the forest floor. All I can do is let my body succumb to the weight of it all, and I imagine myself sinking deep into the earth to live in the bones of our mother. The smoke pouring out of me forms a funnel that lifts to the sky.

Although settler colonialism is always an incomplete project by virtue not just of our resistance but also the resistance and will of creation, we still experience staggering loss, parts of ourselves falling off from the sheer weight of it all. Loss of our loved ones who are taken by intricate processes of genocide. Loss of humanity as the world watches a live-streamed genocide and doesn't act. Loss of our homelands who are opened up, mined, deforested, and polluted. Loss of our children who are taken from us by violence and state-sanctioned removal. Loss of pleasure and our ability to feel whole and full in our bodies that are harmed relentlessly by sexual violence. Loss of presence in our bodies as we drift away from them through the disembodiment that gives us reprieve. The loss is undeniably staggering.

My father speaks at a rally for Anishinaabe and Palestinian children:

"They tried to make me lose.

"Loss of identity, loss of innocence, loss of meaning, loss of family, loss of childhood, loss of language, loss of feeling, loss of community, loss of spirit. Loss of life. Loss of morality.

"Genocide, forced removal, and relocation.

"Trying to change our names. Making it illegal to use our medicines. Making it illegal to dance. Making it illegal to sing. Making it illegal to bury our dead our own way. Making it illegal to birth our babies our way. They tried to make us lose."

But the swirling smoke always remains. Despite the incomprehensible loss and struggle of Indigenous life, the swirling smoke in Indigenous bodies is absolute. As smoke, its medium is immaterial, indescribable, and fleeting yet omnipresent, agentive, and all-encompassing. Settler colonialism reaches out its razor-sharp edge of violence to cut the smoke like it cuts our bodies, but instead, it leaves no mark. Settler colonialism attempts to study the smoke, but it is incapable of comprehending it, and even sometimes of being able to see it.

My father continues:

"I did not lose.

"I gained knowledge of bad and good. Dictatorships. Democracies. Friendships.

"The voice of reason says, stop the atrocities!

"We have to rescue the starving and dying families. We need to get food and aid to the people in Gaza. We are outraged at the brutalities of the regimes."

The smoke beats from my father's chest and swirls up into the sky.

Deep within our bellies, under our rib cages that have been fashioned from generations of our ancestors' heavy and grounded bones, the smoke flickers with the vibrant colours of the universe and the ferocious movement of the great beyond. Deep within our chests, where our homelands grow our sacred empathy, the smoke carries the whispers of our ancestors who call us back into our bodies so that we can be more present in them, so that we can feel, so that we can resist, and so that we can continue to fight for Indigenous life, love, land, and body in our own homelands and beyond.

From within this smoke, the universe breathes creation into us.

From within this smoke, the waters of the universe wash our broken bodies and our spirits tend to our wounds.

I am still lying motionless on the forest floor, but now the land embraces me and begins to sing me a lullaby of sweet and endless creation. She whispers to me, "Let me hold you." The

smoke that swirls deep within my chest begins to rise out of
me, circular wisps that travel from my body up into the sky.
The land whispers, "I am always holding you, I am in your
bones, and I create a garden out of your grief. I am holding
this moment, and I too tremble with the great moan of the
universe. You are not alone in your rage and grief." The smoke
that pours out of me now begins to flicker with pink stardust
and the ancient whispers of ancestors and spirits who give
voice to my pain.

As the land holds me, I slow my breath enough to feel the
smoke rising from my chest. I realize that the smoke did not
come to comfort me in this moment of rupture. My ancestors
were not summoned through my moment of grief and pain.
No, it is the opposite. It is precisely because the smoke swirls
inside me so wildly that I am able to rupture, that I am able
to meet this moment for what it is. I rupture because I can
feel in my body my ancestors' love, rage, and grief as they
witness the ripples of this genocide across the farthest corners
of the universe. I rupture because I feel my homelands tremble with the weight of settler colonialism in my own bones. I
rupture—in my temporary and specific body—because I am
in conversation with all the elements of creation that care
for me, that care for Anishinaabeg, and that care deeply for
Palestinian life, love, justice, and dignity.

The smoke both surrounds me and is me.

Standing beside my father at the rally for Palestine, I speak:

"I owe you our vulnerability when the entire world has been watching yours.

"So I stand beside my father today, and I say, 'Look at what they can never take from us.'

"My father is here, full of love not just for his people but for yours.

"You can starve children and beat them and torture them, but we will never stop loving who we are and the world around us.

"My father is here, full of care just like the tender men of Palestine who are enduring so much, digging children out of the rubble with their bare and bleeding hands.

"And I am here, the daughter of a residential school survivor, with so much love in my body that it teaches me that there is no hierarchy between my children and yours.

"Look at what they can never take from us."

As I speak, smoke pours out of me.

The smoke is always spilling out of me. In my deepest moments of pain, it is there swirling in my chest. When I run far away from my body, it remains emanating out of warm embers that are tended to by ancestors who love me so. When I lie on the forest floor in a moment of ruin, the land holds me and the smoke rises out of my chest to the sky. When I speak to the crowd beside my father, the smoke pouring out of both of us is so tangible that it makes us all weep.

When I was a twelve-year-old girl about to travel far away from my body, the smoke inside me remained. When my father was in residential school being tortured and starved, the smoke inside him was swirling. When my great-great-grandma hid under the bodies of her dead family members in a massacre, the smoke inside her body travelled up into the stars so that the universe could mourn with her. Our ancestors always tend to the fires within our hearts so that the smoke remains. They visit with each other and laugh and joke and pray while they throw kindling on the gentle flames. No amount of violence can ever quell the swirling smoke inside our bodies. We are everything they can never truly touch.

There is no true loss when everything taken from the world continues to live on inside our bodies. Ancestors whisper to me in the night. The waters of my homelands swell and break as I move through my own grief. I touch the great beyond through my flesh, connecting to my responsibilities as an Anishinaabe person who comes from the stars. I teach young people how to feel the swirling smoke inside their bodies and watch them feel loved and held by all our relations. I mark people's bodies with ink and in the rupture bind them to our sacred constellations. I laugh with my daughter and it echoes up to the stars. I weave together futures of Anishinaabe and Palestinian wholeness.

No matter how much violence, how much loss, how much grief, the swirling smoke inside my body will connect me to all that I am and all that I will be. Amid the settler colonial storm, I still have my ability to be whole.

We still have the ability to be whole.

PART II

PART II

Chapter 5

On Wholeness and Spilling Over
Anishinaabe creative practice
and falling in love with all that we are

Spreading paint across canvas is like splashing the world with my own blood. In the most glorious way. All the things that make me who I am dance across the canvas in triumphant harmony. All my ancestors, all my kin, all the moments of my life, translated into colours so vibrant. When a painting is finished, I sit back and revel at the visualization of our expansive love contained within brushstrokes. When I paint, I feel immaculately whole.

Anishinaabe creative practice is the act of dancing with all our relations in order to mark our world. The first part of this framing, dancing with all our relations, signifies the expansive relationality that is at the heart of our art. The second part of this framing, marking our world, signifies that our art is inherently a process of worldbuilding. The true medium of our creative practice is not physical material but rather the relationships that comprise our worldview as Anishinaabe people. Our art begs us to be whole. Our bodies listen. As colours are pulled across canvas, as we dream our art while sitting in the stillness of feeding our children from our bodies, as beads are laid down with the threads of the laughter of our aunties around us, we experience wholeness.

Wholeness, our ability and right to be fully present within our web of relationships that span from birth to death, earth to sky, stars to the great beyond. Wholeness, the ability to convene with everything that we are.

Since time immemorial, Anishinaabeg have cultivated ways to dance wildly with all our relations in order to shape our world. Through ceremony and our own bodies, we are adept at exiting the linearity of time and space to access our ancestors, the spirits, and the low rumble of our expansive universe. Our culture is attuned to our lived reality that includes feeling, seeing, and hearing our ancestors and spirit kin. Our relationships that extend beyond the earthly plane are integral to who we are as a people and allow us to govern ourselves in ways informed by past and future, lovingly cradled by the wisdom of our ancestors and in synchronicity with the totality of the universe.

In the settler colonial world, our culture may be called spiritual, but this label is only necessary in a society that ignores the ancestors and spirits that so viscerally govern the land it has forcefully planted itself upon. Here, to be spiritual is considered whimsical at best, a descriptor that is not assumed to be true or real but rather a phenomenon or spectacle that can initiate a process of othering to be weaponized to support colonial intentions. The concept of spirituality in the settler colony is rooted in hierarchy and compartmentalization. Within the realm of this constructed spirituality, there are so-called experts or leaders who climb the spiritual hierarchy and obtain spiritual authority. Within the realm of this constructed spirituality, compartmental-ization rules—to be spiritual is to exist solely in the realm of the sacred.

Taking note of the colonial construction of the concept of spirituality allows me to clearly step away from the stereotyp-ical, limiting, and inaccurate representations of Indigenous spirituality that dominate mainstream consciousness when discussing Anishinaabe body, ceremony, and creative prac-tice. Indigenous peoples have always borne the brunt of spiritual stereotypes that confine us to the tropes of the wise medicine man or shaman, which are deep-rooted tactics of dehumanization. From an Anishinaabe perspective, to be spiritual is simply to be human. There is no spiritual hierar-chy because everyone lives out their own relationships with their ancestors and spirit kin. There is no confinement of spirituality to the sacred because we are in constant conver-sation with the great beyond through our bodies, in every moment of every mundane or transcendent day.

When I convene with my ancestors, I do not have to be in a smoky lodge with sacred drumming all around me. When I converse with my spirit helpers, I do not have to be deep in the bush walking in stillness. These communions happen amid the everyday and in so many different ways precisely because our bodies are the technology that allows us to dance with all our relations. Because our bodies extend beyond the physical, they allow us to touch the great beyond and dance with our ancestors. And because our bodies are unique, how each of us experiences this is radically different from one another. There is no monolithic spiritual experience that makes us Anishinaabe. There is everything but the monolith, and that is what makes being Anishinaabe so beautiful.

Sometimes, a painting is seamlessly bound to the present, past, and future simultaneously. Sometimes, it makes no sense in the beginning and all the sense at the end. When I started working on my painting the place before birth, *I didn't even really know why; a cool concept, at best. As I started painting, so much boiled up in me: My mother. My father. In Anishinaabe culture we sit in the stars and choose our parents. We see our whole life ahead of us and we consent to it.*

When we participate in ceremony or make art, we are using our bodies. Both ceremony and art use the body as a technology that allows us to rupture the here and now in order to touch the great beyond. Although both practices look radically different, I have felt similarities between the two along a spectrum. There are moments when I paint where I feel in direct conversation with my ancestors. At times, I have even laughed out loud. There are also moments when I paint where I am fully and utterly my human self, floating through my own earthbound experiences. And then there are explicit moments when the art becomes the ceremony itself. It is here where I feel that distinct sharpness in the air, the rupturing of time and space not just through my own body but in the space around it, opening up enough to hear the whispers of the universe beside me.

When I experience this explicit feeling of ceremony when I am tattooing, painting, or beading, I know that whatever I am working on is in direct conversation with something much larger than me. For me, making art is a methodology of wholeness, a way to come back into my body and dance with all our relations. Along this entire spectrum, I glimpse wholeness.

Although ceremony and art often intersect explicitly for me, this may not be true for others. We all have vastly different bodies that filter our experiences accordingly. We also all carry different responsibilities that alter how we respond to, and convene with, the spirit world. Sharing my personal relationship to creative practice is not to say that art is ceremony, but rather to demonstrate one way in which our art is informed by all our relations, including those that extend beyond this world. In an Anishinaabe worldview, no matter how or what an artist creates, it is undeniably shaped by all their relationships. Again, pushing against the colonial construct of spirituality, our art does not have to contain so-called spiritual content to be informed by the spirit world. Much like there is no need to label Anishinaabe culture as spiritual because it is simply our lived reality, there is no need to label Anishinaabe art as spiritual for the same reason.

Our art is always lovingly guided by the hands of our ancestors. Our art is always pulsing with the swirling, starry sky. Our art has always been one of our central methods for accessing that holy place of the great beyond, the great return to dancing with all our relations. Our art has always allowed us to be whole.

As I continued to paint the place before birth, I discovered an abnormal area on my cervix and had to get a biopsy. It was scary and tender. When I returned to painting some days later, I wept and was able to access a new kind of vulnerability. My womb, wounded, sat inside my mother's in the place before birth and understood. When I painted, I laughed out loud because the painting felt like a gift from my ancestors to do this work, seamlessly interacting with my outside life and physical body. It was the furthest from loneliness I have ever felt. We can never truly be lonely as Anishinaabe people because our ancestors are always with us.

Anishinaabe art is so full of colour. I weep at the vibrancy of our lives. I weep at the depth of our creative practice. Colour does not simply signify the visual colours we all know; colour also tethers us to the spiritual realm and the place beyond time. Anishinaabeg use colours to mark our specific relationships within the spirit realm and to communicate our positionalities with our spirit kin. To be full of colour is to be many things all at once—past, present, and future. To be full of colour is to be incomprehensible to the dull and flat settler colonial world. Our art cannot be contained within the visual, even when it comes to colour. I fall to my knees at the vibrancy of our lives.

Settler colonialism, always an attempted removal of our bodies from the land, attempts to contain our colour and still our shifting and complex bodies into categories of control. When they flooded my homelands, the water became muddied. When they harmed my father in residential school, they tried to make him turn grey. But everything they do is always limited to the physical. They can never reach our true colour. When my homelands were flooded, the animals worked hard to restore the water's colour, and now it shines so blue. When my father was taken, he poured rainbow colours from his tears. They can never touch the vibrancy of our lives.

Three months after my biopsy, I was pregnant. I was painting the place before birth *while Giizik sat in the place before birth, looking down at her life and consenting to it. I laughed out loud again.*

Anishinaabe creative practice is rooted in a deep and expansive relationality that mirrors our own webs of relationality. From the web of the immediate family outward to the larger community, our homelands, clans, helpers, animals, fish, insects, elements, spirits, stars, and ancestors. We are relentlessly enveloped in love, care, and guidance from all elements of creation. Our worldview recognizes that our knowledge and our art are informed by these relationships. Understanding our knowledge as expansively relational honours the collectivity of life.

In an Anishinaabe worldview, every single person and being contributes to creative practice regardless of whether they participate in its explicit production. The people who physically create—the beadworkers, painters, carvers, birch workers, poets, and dancers—do so in conversation with the relationships around them that make them whole. Those who do not physically create—the auntie, the grandmother sitting in her chair, the moon, the muskrat, and the beating sun—still participate in the creative practice that so tenderly learns from and considers them. Our knowledge and our art are everything beyond the concept of the individual.

Whereas other forms of communication can encapsulate our earthly experiences that are governed by linear time and space, art is one of the only forms of communication that can reach into the great beyond and allow us to share spiritual knowledge with our broader communities. Art is knowledge transmission in non-literal and non-didactic ways, making it an integral form of communication. For this reason, creative practice has always been foundational to our systems of governance, allowing us to build our world in alignment with all our relations, whether earthbound or beyond. We are a people planted firmly on the earth, yet our hearts house the stars that we come from. The ways that we govern ourselves reflect this. The intersection of Anishinaabe creative practice and governance solidifies our art as a practice of worldbuilding. Our creative practice is not oriented toward aesthetics or success but rather toward the very material marking of the world around us in conversation with all the relationships that comprise who we are. Creative practice is a responsibility to build our world.

Our art, like ceremony and our bodies, is a way to dance with all our relations and then share that knowledge in order to mark our world. Our art, in its most basic sense, is expressing knowledge that is informed through expansive relationality in order to build the world in beauty and liberation, reverence and justice. The intent of our art is to splash the world with our wild and uninhibited relationality, colours strewn across landscapes that birth swirling spirits that whisper visions for a more just future. Because Anishinaabe art is oriented toward a responsibility for worldbuilding, the primary focus is not on production but rather on affecting the world itself. The value of our art is thus not limited to output but is within the processes that will carry us toward these futures, which are often not contained within the visual or material.

Our art might exist in the form of a product—when we bead or paint—but our art might also exist in the non-material realm—when we dream or scheme, organize or govern. Our art might exist in the form of a product temporarily before passing away back into the spirit world, its message carried forward in the hearts of those who witnessed it. Anishinaabe art is simultaneously fleeting and omnipresent. It is many things all at once, spilling over, unable to be defined by product or medium, or even by time and space.

This expansive conception of creative practice is incomprehensible to the settler colonial world of hyperproduction and individualism. In the settler colonial world, the role of the artist is limited to the act of dreaming, which is articulated through a form of production, ignoring our responsibilities to materially change the world around us in conversation with the art we are creating. Artists are encouraged to dream within the limits of the settler colonial imaginary and are rewarded when they do not challenge our oppressive conditions. Rewarding artists solely based on their production invisibilizes and devalues community-based work that puts dreams into action.

My art is more than the paintings I create. When I create a painting, I might be dreaming up new worlds for us, but my work cannot end there. I have a deep obligation to materially change the world so that the dream can become a reality. For this reason, my personal arts practice has always been in conjunction with my contributions to community. When I visualize the love my ancestors have for my body through a painting, I am doing so in conjunction with helping Indigenous youth feel the same way about their bodies. When I marked my ankles with ink, I was doing so to mark a commitment to dancing. When I painted a future where Anishinaabeg and Palestinians were free and whole, it led me to mobilize a delegation of Palestinian organizers to visit my homelands. The dreaming and the living out of the dream, no matter how hard, cannot be separated. Artists have a responsibility not just to dream but also to do.

If Anishinaabe art has to be defined, it is the practice of spilling over. Beyond the confines of linear time, the necessity of production, and the non-living canvas, Anishinaabe art spills over these confines with the force of whitewater over rapids. Our art, the place where our ancestors dance, an explosion of colour so vibrant it breaks the here and now. Our art, the place where Anishinaabe knowledge lives and breathes, a fleeting moment in the cosmic flow of creation. Our art, contained not just in paint and beads, but also in stardust, our own blood, the clear water of a still lake, and the voices of our ancestors. Our art, the building of our world such that we are all free and whole. Our art, the pathway to our wholeness.

I painted the residential school that my father went to. Painstakingly, I traced the exact infrastructure that

represents the utter terror and confinement of my people.
Harsh and straight lines, repetitive boxes, different shades of
grey and beige. It took me a long time. And then, I returned
with the colour they could never touch—splattering neon
pink and the turquoise of Gitchee Gumee, spilling out the
ancestors and spirits they could never contain, the babies yet
to be born, the futures untold. I visualized how we are always
spilling over the compartmentalizations of their violence.
Like a tidal wave of creation, we are everything they can
never have.

My father is one of the strongest examples I have of
what Anishinaabe knowledge and creative practice looks
like—embodied and agentive. He survived residential
school through his artwork, and then spent his life selling his carvings and paintings on busy street corners in
urban centres. At times, he traversed gallery spaces, but
mostly he remained on the streets. My father never taught
me how to paint; he didn't have to. Our art is passed down
intergenerationally, fed to us through the loving hands of
our ancestors. Our art is passed down in spirit, not in skill
and aesthetics. What my father did teach me was how to
orient myself as an Anishinaabe person, and how to insist
that our worldview remain firmly planted in my own body.
How we orient ourselves is who we are speaking to, who
we are listening to, and where our energy is directed. My
father always oriented himself not toward the gallery, the
inclusion, the palatable, or the career, but rather toward
the stars that we come from, the low moan of creation, and
the rumbling of life.

To carve a black ash tree, we need to sleep for days in the bush. At night, we will study the constellations and line our bodies up with the stars that we come from. During the day, we will use our bare hands to move the earth around the tree that was struck by lightning. It doesn't really matter what the carving looks like in the end. What matters is everything that wills it to be, everything that holds it in place.

Although my father didn't teach me how to paint, he did instill in me our Anishinaabe relationships to creative practice. He taught me that we are responsible for the relationships we are a part of, grounding me in an arts practice that always foregrounds my material contributions to community in addition to any production of visual work. The centring of art as a practice of worldbuilding and deep responsibility necessitates a critical interrogation of the settler colonial context that harms our bodies, lands, and communities. Our worldbuilding takes place within the violent and hostile context of settler colonialism that is intent on our destruction. As artists, we have a deep responsibility to resist and transcend our settler colonial conditions, and to see this responsibility as existing outside of our own lived experiences, families, and communities.

My father taught me how to care for our spirit kin through our art. My father taught me how to care for our bodies using our art. My father taught me how to care for other people and communities using our art. As such, I have always directed my energy toward understanding and charting settler colonialism as part of my responsibility as an artist who wishes to transcend these realities. But it is hard to wade through the settler colonial matrix as an artist. Anishinaabe art itself is embedded within the Western art world, and must contend with the logics and power dynamics of colonialism.

Settler colonialism, as a force of compartmentalization, seeks to separate art from life, disrupting the complex and beautiful threads of creative practice that flow across the universe. In the settler colonial world, art becomes strictly an aesthetic product oriented toward success within the capitalist conditions it exists within. From the Western perspective, art becomes practices like painting and drawing, music and dance, but only insofar as we are directly contributing to some iteration of a product of these practices. Art becomes a box, separated from the expansive relationality of the universe that birthed it. The purpose of this compartmentalization has multiple dimensions.

First and foremost, it is part of the larger compartmentalization of the human being from the web of creation they exist within that lays the groundwork for the primary unit of settler colonialism: the individual. The establishment of vapid individualism supports capitalism while preventing people from accessing their internal knowledge, feeling a sense of belonging and purpose, and forging relationships of mutual dependency that can reduce state reliance. When we remove art from its relationality and process, we demand that the artist create from outside their web of creation, following the logics of the individualism that is the heart of settler colonialism.

The Western art world, following in the footsteps of the settler colonial infrastructure that birthed it, operates according to hierarchy. The units of this hierarchy are the constructs of skill and clout, which function as the measure of value in the settler colonial art world. In this context, skill is a construct in which value is applied to measure creativity rather arbitrarily. The Western art world is divided into experts and amateurs, skilled artists and beginners, those who "just have it" and those who don't. Here, I use the term *skill* to denote something different from mastery, which I think of as a more functional term that places value on learning the practical aspects of a craft. Skill, however, has a shifting meaning beyond mastery of a craft, often assigning value to art that is palatable and profitable, highly subjective and governed by colonial logics. The construction of clout emerges with the idea of an expert or visionary that is supported by the Western art world's ability to control the systems of value surrounding art. There is now a social hierarchy supported by material power. If you can control who is considered an expert, who is an artist, and what is considered good art, then you can generate an industry of control that will support the colonial project. Of course, there are many ruptures to these systems. Many artists have existed, and continue to exist, on the margins of this world, creating work that is so powerful that it exceeds these conditions, but these are still the conditions it must transcend.

In the settler colonial world, you can climb the imposed hierarchy to be considered an artist or expert by creating work that is deemed valuable within this system. Capitalism wills it to be so. What will be considered valuable art will be decided by the constructs of skill and clout, which are always ultimately oriented toward the settler colony. Creative practice is taken away from process and becomes the product. The immateriality inherent to creative practice—the relationship-building and the worldbuilding—is not only erased but is also devalued and even punished within the settler colonial context. There is no value ascribed to work that does not yield a product in the settler colonial world.

Settler colonialism works hard to ensure that its art industry follows its logics of compartmentalization, hierarchy, and control. Through the compartmentalization of artist from their web of creation, and product from expansive process, the artist becomes an individual who will create products that then determine their worth within the system of capitalism. Artists are rewarded for their complicity within the structures of settler colonialism, receiving fame and monetary gain for visionary thinking that challenges mainstream perspectives enough to move people without threatening the material conditions of settler colonialism. Artists who choose to operate on the margins will largely not experience these rewards, and will have to find ways to support themselves and define their own sense of artistic value.

Settler colonialism does not want art to bind people to their web of relationships because this enables people to resist and dismantle the oppression they face. Settler colonialism does not want art to make people whole, reminding them of their homelands and the loving embrace of their ancestors through their own bodies. Settler colonialism most certainly does not want art to bring the individual back to the collective, where they are reunited with deep purpose and communal responsibility that lives outside the settler colony.

Anishinaabe relationships to creative practice stand in stark contrast to the Western approaches to art that dominate our lived reality. Anishinaabe creative practice both spills over and demolishes the structural violence of settler colonialism—it is both attentive to the destruction of settler colonialism and oriented toward all our relations that exist in the still night sky and deep in the red earth. Anishinaabe art *is* the practice of spilling over—undefinable, elusive, agentive, and fleeting. Our art is ungovernable, sovereign; like the rushing river of creation, it is unstoppable. It is all the fragmented moments that bring our hand to the paintbrush—the way the moon hung in the sky that night, what our ancestors whispered in the stillness of the morning light, our helpers and the trembling land beneath our feet.

We are always spilling over. They have never been able to contain us, all our spirits bubbling up in the colourful paint that marks canvas and body, land and sky. We are bursting with colour they can never comprehend.

I paint my body in ecstasy. The blood of my ancestors rushes out of my body to meet the river that calls me back to my own wholeness. On each leg, my bear guardians protect the sovereignty of my pleasure. So much is spilling out of me when I feel good. My body flickers under the moon who caresses me so gently. My father's body. My mother's body. I insist on wholeness for them too. So much is spilling out of each paint stroke—the waterways of my flooded homelands, the laughter of my ancestors, the trembling delight of the great beyond.

My visual art practice has always felt as natural as breathing. I have painted and built worlds around me as an inherent component to my identity. But as an Anishinaabe artist who honours my worldview in all its expansive entirety within a context that wants to assimilate or destroy that worldview, I largely operate at the margins of the Western art world. This art world often cannot comprehend, nor adequately care for, my art and all that it contains. When my art has been shown within the walls of the gallery I have always asked myself, *What does this actually offer me and my community? What does it mean to show my work in a space where many of my relatives feel uncomfortable? What does it mean when my dad and uncle are stared at pervasively on a busy opening night? What relationships did this exhibition actually make or nurture?*

Eventually, I stopped orienting myself solely toward galleries and institutions and focused that energy on my creative practice itself. Now I mostly share my work through social media and am selective and intentional about my participation in exhibitions. Orienting myself toward my own community and away from the opportunities that garner more visibility, success, and monetary reward constitutes a sacrifice to my arts career. These choices render my arts practice less valid, less comprehensible, and less valued within the Western art world, yet orienting myself toward my community is my responsibility as an Anishinaabe artist.

My creative practice is made up of the practices of both dreaming and doing. I think of the act of dreaming as things like painting, beading, writing, and all the ways we are able to convene with our relations in order to dream up new worlds. I think of the practice of doing as our material contributions to building a better and more liberatory world for all our relations. The settler colonial compartmentalization of dreaming from doing attempts to remove the artist from their responsibility to build a better world. As an artist, I must not just dream but also do. The Western art world entirely invisibilizes this approach to creative practice. On paper, I am an artist who has slow and inconsistent production, who lacks specialization, and who does not have a trajectory of exhibition and gallery success. On paper, I am all over the map—youth work, anti-colonial education, painting, tattooing, writing, institutional harm reduction, and arts programming.

As an artist who not only creates physical artworks but also insists on including material acts of worldbuilding as part of my practice, I find that my community-based work is an impediment to my legitimacy as an artist in the Western context. My community-based work is considered irrelevant to my role as an artist, which means I appear to be an inconsistent, disjointed, and unfocused artist on paper, missing out on many opportunities for success in the settler colonial world.

From an Anishinaabe perspective, I am living out my responsibilities as an artist who honours art as the act of dreaming and doing, materially shaping the world to usher in the dreaming that I do through my visual work. From an Anishinaabe understanding of art, I am living out my responsibilities of what it means to be Anishinaabe and an artist.

My main contribution to building the world around

me has been to work with Indigenous youth through arts programming that honours Indigenous relationships to creative practice. I created the Indigenous Youth Residency program, an intensive and paid artist residency for Native youth ages twelve to twenty-four. This program developed pedagogy and curriculum from Anishinaabe ways of being and creating, ensuring that Indigenous youth could embody their culturally relevant approaches to creative practice while learning about settler colonialism, resistance, and Indigenous brilliance. I ran the inaugural program out of the Art Gallery of Ontario, and since then it has run in Thunder Bay for eight years. This work also includes long-term mentorship opportunities for Indigenous youth, and I have mentored two youth over three years to help them learn how to develop and run similar programming.

The program hires six youth and runs for six weeks full time. For the first four weeks, we follow an anti-colonial and relational curriculum that explores relationships to self, community, homelands, and ancestors. During these four weeks, we are doing the heavy lifting of learning about settler colonialism while exploring relationship-building as artistic practice itself. We work with Elders, knowledge keepers, and artists who complement our curriculum, and we sit in circle with one another and share our lived experiences. For the fifth week, we take a one-week camping trip together. For the sixth week, youth are in the studio creating a final piece that summarizes everything they have learned, and these works are exhibited at an art gallery. We have a huge opening night where youth invite their families and communities to witness the work that has been done. I give a speech that honours each specific youth and their gifts. We feast together and celebrate.

The foundational methodology I developed for this program is to honour Anishinaabe knowledge and creative practice as inherently and expansively relational. The program only works with six youth at a time over a long period in order to have ample space for deep and meaningful relationships not just between participants but also with Elders, knowledge keepers, and community members. Furthermore, rather than focusing on mastery, skill, or aesthetic, we focus on relationship-building as art-making itself, exploring relationships to self, body, homelands, and community as entry points to our creative practice. How do we feel our ancestors within our bodies? How do we relate to our homelands when we are away from them? What is our experience of settler colonialism in our bodies and lands? We explore these questions collectively and individually while building deep relationships that make many of us family.

The curriculum of the program is oriented around exploring our relationships in the context of settler colonialism. In an ideal world, we would explore our relationships to self, body, homelands, community, and ancestors in peace, but in this world we must contend with how settler colonialism impacts these relationships. Indigenous youth deeply understand colonialism already because they have to live through it every day, but giving them specific tools and language to better name and understand colonialism can be life-changing.

We learn about the structures of settler colonialism— cisheteropatriarchy, ableism, ageism, white supremacy, fatphobia, and capitalism. We learn about the strategies of settler colonialism—assimilation, genocide, and dispossession. We learn about the history and contemporary manifestations of colonialism—residential schools, the foster care system, the crisis of missing and murdered Indigenous women, girls, Two-Spirit, and trans people, the pass system, mining, mercury poisoning, flooding, forced sterilization, and so forth. Throughout the program, we remain oriented around the definition of colonialism as the removal of Indigenous bodies from our homelands in order to clear the land for settler occupation and expansion. We understand that all our realities of harm and violence are the intentional impacts of a system that, by necessity, must enact our destruction. This mode of thinking is revolutionary and allows youth to realize that they are not at fault for their disconnections and struggles but rather the state is.

The program also rejects the hierarchy inherent to Western arts education. There are so few paid opportunities for young people to access cultural or arts-based programs. When there are paid opportunities, they are often governed by the social hierarchies of who is or isn't deserving of a job dependent on resumé and extracurriculars. For this program, we interviewed youth in order to meet them, see how they might work with one another, and consider their degree of need for the program. Rather than hiring youth who already considered themselves artists or who were excelling in certain areas, we hired youth who exist on the margins because of settler colonialism. Youth in care; youth with unstable housing; trans, queer, and Two-Spirit youth; youth engaged in the carceral system; and youth without access to culture were valued for their lived experience. Our art is a responsibility to worldbuild, and we must learn from the voices of our community members who are so often denied access and dignity. And so we would ask ourselves, "Who needs the connection within this program? Who is being excluded elsewhere? Who might work well together?" Each iteration hired six amazing Indigenous artists, and the demand was always overwhelmingly high, signalling the need for this type of program.

As the facilitator, I took on the role of a guide rather than expert or authority figure. I made an intentional effort to be more like a friend with solid boundaries than a conventional teacher who assumes superiority. We used the sharing circle as a foundational pedagogical tool that dismantles hierarchy within a space of learning. When we are in-circle, every single person puts their knowledge in the circle. No one's knowledge is more important than another's, and all the knowledge is rooted in our lived experience. Every single day we would have multiple circles—one to start and end the day and one to accompany our more structured lessons. This allowed me to teach youth in a more conventional way when imparting specific language and tools around an analysis of settler colonialism, and then ground this teaching in lived experience. Importantly, I used a methodology of self-vulnerability. In the circles I would intentionally share pieces of my relevant lived experiences related to settler colonialism in order to complement the teaching. Another way of saying this is that I have so much love for our young people that I am willing to give so much of myself to them.

The youth taught me how to care for my own body. Over the years, they kept reminding me to show as much love and care for myself as I do for them. I was always giving, always rupturing myself so that they could see my blood and grief and pain, so that it could help them transcend theirs. The smoke always calls me to be whole, but I struggle with my desire, my yearning, my ability to feel deserving of my own wholeness. The seeds of inferiority, worthlessness, and self-hatred that colonialism plants in our bodies kept me from loving myself for so long, but the youth insisted I let my love spill over onto my own body. Out of me poured paintings of my body feeling whole, a visual pathway of care and love. Later, I began to find the words to weave curriculum about feelings of the body into the youth program more overtly, to talk about worthlessness and our bodies. Our art is all of this. Not just the paintings, but also the dancing of paintbrushes and sitting in circles, crying on the floor and the moon stroking my back. The young people taught me how to become whole.

When I started this work, I did not know of any other art programs for Indigenous youth that seriously considered Indigenous methodologies of creative practice. To this day, I still do not know of any. Although there are lots of programs that teach youth how to bead or paint, or even learn about our culture and cultural arts practices, there is still a lack of programming that does these things through our ways of being and knowing. How we do things is just as important as what we are doing, and I remain committed to helping youth reclaim the sacred smoke inside them when they're creating art.

I also understand why these opportunities do not exist for Indigenous youth in the context of settler colonialism. The Western art world is still unable to comprehend Indigenous creative practice, and furthermore, our art is often threatening to its hegemony. This means that running a program like this is inherently exhausting and full of harm when interacting with institutional contexts. The scope of the relational work inherent to this program took every ounce of my being. Sitting in deep relation with Indigenous youth and exploring topics of colonialism requires boundless love, commitment, and sacrifice, which are big asks of people trying to navigate their own survival within capitalism and colonialism. I understand that this program is specific to my own skill set, gifts, and capacities, and I value the work that others do in alignment with their own approaches.

Running this program within various institutional contexts taught me a lot about the limits of genuine decolonization within the institution. Although art galleries are often positioned as neutral and liberal spaces, they are still a unit of settler colonial architecture that is governed by its logics and structures of oppression. I ran the inaugural iteration of the program in one of the largest art galleries in the country, where I witnessed the colonial machinery of the Western arts world in all its ferocity. Although the institution initially welcomed my presence, there was no tolerance for work that operated outside the confines of Western arts education, and I quickly understood how deeply threatening my work was. The institution could not tolerate that I was going to work with only six youth at a time over a long period, insisting on a quantitative approach to youth programming with large numbers and short programs. The institution was enraged that I would even consider paying youth for their time and expertise, and I was quite literally yelled at for even considering this. When I brought Indigenous youth into the institution, they were met with hostility, surveillance, and racism.

I fought through these tensions in order to protect the sovereignty of my work and the wholeness of Anishinaabe art that the institution had been so keen to include as part of their stated dedication to decolonization. All these tensions existed because the work I was doing was deeply threatening to the pillars of settler colonialism that uphold the Western arts world. The operating logics of the institution were threatened by the living embodiment of Anishinaabe creative practice. This is how fragile they are. A single Native woman quietly working with six Indigenous youth in the basement of a multi-million-dollar institution was powerful enough to make them tremble.

Working through these tensions, though exhausting and dehumanizing, allowed me to chart the intricacies of how Indigenous labour is co-opted, exploited, and demonized within institutions. In the era of reconciliation, institutions are hiring more Indigenous people in superficially inclusive ways that skirt the material changes in power and privilege that are actually the foundation of meaningful inclusion. Institutions can thus optically benefit from their hiring decisions yet remain rooted in their commitment to the structures of settler colonialism that harm the bodies they are attempting to include. When I first entered the gallery, my love for and commitment to Indigenous youth were treated as exploitable resources and a means to extract my labour. In my desire to make the institution a better place for Indigenous youth, I was coerced into doing the fraught work of decolonizing an institution that did not want to change. I was pulled in many directions, my labour often co-opted by the institution in order to obtain grants and visibility on my behalf without me reaping any of the material rewards. I watched myself become a non-human entity within the institution, a generalized Native person with no name and no personhood.

When I reached the limits of my own exploitation, my labour became demonized within the institution. When my love for Indigenous youth led me to erect boundaries around my own labour, I became threatening, devious, and unsettling to the institution rather than an exploitable resource. The institution was no longer able to commodify and exploit my love as an Indigenous woman when that same love was now holding boundaries. I insisted that Native youth not be racially profiled in the institution. I insisted that there be transparent pathways for incident reporting and accountability. I insisted that Native youth be paid for the job I was hiring them for. My love was no longer seen as a means to extract my unpaid labour, but a deeply threatening force capable of spilling over the hierarchies that the institution works so hard to maintain. Instead of being treated like a decolonization expert, I was now demonized and considered worthless, amateur, and ridiculous. When the institution confronted my refusal to cede control and be commodified, I was labelled and treated as a deviant threat.

It was an exhausting year, but I persisted. I ran the youth

program and marvelled at the worldbuilding we collectively enacted together. And I left with such abundant knowledge of the inner workings of the institution in terms of Indigenous labour co-optation and the limits of institutional decolonization.

From this point onward, I developed an autonomous space model for my artistic programming that clearly delineated the limited role of the institution within the program. On the one hand, we don't need institutions at all, considering they are the building blocks of settler colonialism and replicate so many of the structures we seek to transcend. On the other hand, we are owed sovereign space and material resources from the institutions that occupy stolen land. For young people, institutions can also yield a form of legitimacy and validation that can be incredibly powerful. The ability for youth to consider themselves artist residents at a mainstream gallery, the ability for youth to feel like they belong at an arts institution, and the ability for youth to put this designation on their resumés was still something I valued enough to justify working with institutions.

For the following years, I worked with the Thunder Bay Art Gallery through this autonomous space model. They provided physical meeting space and exhibition space as part of their inherent responsibility to the people whose land and art they commodify, and that was it. There was no collaboration within the program, no attempt to control it, and no ownership of the work. As trust was built, my relationship with them deepened and we were able to collaborate outside of the methodologies of the program itself. This approach allowed me to protect the sovereignty of my work, give youth access to an institution that holds so much of our artwork, and ensure I was able to direct most of my energy toward the youth themselves.

When we make art, we dance with the swirling smoke inside our bodies. The smoke brings our youth home. The smoke calls our youth back into their bodies and wraps them in their inherent wholeness. The voices of our ancestors whisper that they are so loved and cherished. In a place that is quite literally attempting to kill and harm them, they never get to hear that they are loved and cherished. I love and cherish you. Our art and the swirling smoke inside of our bodies holds us in reverence for all that we are.

By the final week of the program, the young people would have taught me so much about what it means to move love through our bodies, across our homelands, and to one another amid the settler colonial storm. Like releasing the dam that submerges so many of our homelands, our words and tears flowed in a purifying release. This was the week when we talked about our shame—shame for our bodies, shame for the faults in our communities, shame for our parents, shame for being Native. Crucially, this was the week when we contextualized our shame as a colonial construct manufactured to obscure the source of our harm in order to relegate it to individual and internalized blame. To talk about our shame, while charting the larger architecture of colonialism, is to redirect that blame toward the structures of colonialism that have worked so hard to harm us. We charted settler colonialism so intimately through our bodies, artwork, and stories that we now understood where to put the blame. Our disconnection is inevitable in the settler colonial context that attempts to remove us from our homelands—disconnection of self from body, of body from land, from parents, from community, from culture. But our disconnection is not our fault. And our disconnection is never fully complete.

Our shame is not ours to carry. In one collective moment, we walk away from our shame. As we release our shame, there is more space for the smoke inside us to swirl—all the whispers of our ancestors who adore us, our homelands who pulse through our veins, and our true sense of purpose and responsibility fill up the bodies of our young people with the certainty of all that they are. In one collective moment, we remember what is contained within our bodies, in absolution. Our ancestors live in our flesh, and drum in synchronicity with our beating hearts. Our homelands pulse through our veins with the same tenacity as the singing rapids of our waterways. Our spirit kin visit us through the smoke that is irrevocably and wholly inside us, binding us to our responsibilities from the great beyond. Our bodies contain everything we need within them. Nothing can truly be lost when our bodies swirl with stardust and the low moan of creation. Settler colonialism cannot fully reach us. There are things they can never touch and things they can never reach. Despite the disconnections and the violent infrastructure that surround our bodies, we are everything they could never even dream of. Indigenous youth deserve to feel this. They just need the reminder. They just need someone to say, "I love you, and all of creation does too. Look at what is inside of you."

It is one of the greatest honours of my life to stand along-side the youth and learn from them. As much as I remind them of the swirling smoke inside their bodies, so too do they ignite my smoke, and together we become whole. It is such a beautiful thing, amid the colonial chaos, to dance with all our relations together, to lay our stories down in the circle and carry the load for one another, to dream worlds of fullness into reality through the relationships we create. It is such a beautiful thing to witness the unfaltering love that Indigenous youth continue to have for their bodies and families and homelands and ancestors, despite the odds. It is such a beautiful thing to watch love so effortlessly pour out of me—I will rupture myself through blood and sweat and tears a million times if it can help them be whole for even a moment. It is such a beautiful thing to glimpse such glorious futures through the tenacity and will of these young people.

At the end of the day, my job is so very easy. All I have to do is hold space for young people that is filled with care and respect, whisper to them that I love them unconditionally, and demonstrate with my actions that I do. The rest flows like the river of creation, futures unfolding before our very eyes. We live in a world where Native youth yearn to feel loved. We live in a world where Native youth do not feel loved by the world that is trying to destroy them. When I whisper, "I love you," our collective ancestors breathe a sigh of relief and fade into the starry night sky.

Our art is like falling in love, a love that traverses the great beyond and touches star, ancestor, water, and tree. The soft pulse of creation within the palms of our hands. Finding each other in the cold and endless night to embrace in the settler colonial storm.

Anishinaabe art is the practice of spilling over. Undefinable, rebellious, momentous, and full of impact, it spills over the harsh compartmentalizations that settler colonialism works so hard to maintain. Full of colour that exists beyond the physical, we paint our worlds into justice and liberation with brushstroke and footstep, calm and sturdy voices, and the echoes of our ancestors' whispers. When we create, we are brought into our bodies; we are whole, dancing wildly with all the elements of creation that make us who we are. When we create, we are full like the moon that watches over us so intently, gifting us the dreams of a better future for all. Like falling in love, our creative practice is the relational reclamation of our sacred web of creation, and we bask in our cherishment as the universe delights in our existence. Like falling in love, our creative practice brings us wholeness.

Chapter 6

On Wholeness and Worldbuilding
Parenting with our whole bodies
in order to build the worlds our children need

I was standing by a still lake, not a ripple to be found on its surface. I saw two bears approaching in the distance, walking deliberately and steadily toward me. I felt scared but not panicked, and I slowly lowered myself into the lake to hide myself from their view. One of the bears approached the shore and started swimming toward me. As it reached me, it opened its mouth and ever so gently took my arm in its teeth, pulling me back to shore as it swam. The other bear received me at the bank. The two bears escorted me down a long trail, walking with purpose.

I woke up on a crisp morning in January 2020 in a heightened state of awareness. I had just had the most beautiful dream, and I closed my eyes to bring it back into my mind's eye. Without hesitation, I knew—not only was I pregnant, but I was reunited, I was whole. I played the vivid dream over and over in my head while I felt the soft bed hold my body. Although this pregnancy was completely unexpected, I felt so calm. I also felt overwhelmingly honoured to be chosen, not just to be this spirit's mother but also to receive a dream of such generous clarity.

The bears led me to a smoke-filled lodge. I lost my body in the lodge, dissolving into a particle of dust. I swirled around the lodge as if I was a part of the smoke, my only sense of physicality the inertia and momentum of the swirling sensation. It was dark and the smoke was dense. I began to ascend to the top of the lodge where it opened into the sky.

I woke up on a morning in late August in a state of discomfort, tossing and turning. It was 4:30 a.m. My belly was big and round, but Giizik was not due until mid-September and birth was not yet on my mind. In the stillness of the night, I got up and started pacing as the pain became immediate and intense. I managed to remain calm and ran myself a bath, but by the time it was ready, I was unable to stay still or get in. I turned off the faucet and looked down at my trembling hands, feeling nauseous with pain. I sat down and acknowledged that she was coming. Although it was so early, and my kin weren't beside me as I had planned, I felt calm and certain.

I called my midwife and she told me to try to relax and get some sleep. She said that I was likely in early labour, which can take hours. I was too stoic and self-reliant to make her understand otherwise. I thought, *Well, if this is early labour, I cannot even fathom what active labour will feel like.* But the pain was so intense that any thoughts or feelings didn't have space to stay. I began to time my contractions and reviewed them with incredulity—three minutes between a contraction, and then the next one two minutes, and the next one, one minute. A large rush of blood flooded my pyjama pants.

I called my midwife again and she told me to very calmly but very quickly drive the thirty minutes to the Thunder Bay hospital, even though I had wanted to give birth at home. Despite this being a potential emergency, I have never felt more calm and resolved in my life. No room for any worries or doubts, just me and my body. I woke up Giizik's dad, and as we walked to the car, I looked up at the night sky and I could hear Gitchee Gumee lapping on the shore. I thought, *No matter how hard it gets, it doesn't matter as long as I have this.* The stars smiled back at me in adoration.

As we drove I was in complete agony. I was unable to move, forced into stillness. When a contraction came, I had no reprieve and every bump of the car made me quiver. It was a silent ride so that I could focus.

When we made it to the hospital, I used the bathroom immediately and I was already bearing down, my body ready to push. I didn't tell the midwives this, and instead, I was utterly my usual awkward self, apologizing for being unable to answer their questions during contractions and keeping up an unnecessarily jolly tone. The midwife checked my cervix and looked shocked. She told me I was fully dilated and that I needed to start pushing immediately. Everything was crystal clear in that moment—it was just me and my body.

I floated out of the lodge and became myself again, reunited with my body, except now I wasn't alone. I was with a being. We were slowly rising into the sky together—first passing through clouds, and then watching as the earth became smaller and smaller below us. Then we made it all the way to the stars. There were pink galaxies all around us—stardust that shimmered with ancient purple and intricate constellations that endlessly surrounded us. The being flickered between many forms. They were a baby, but they were not just one person, and they kept changing and shifting as we floated through the stars.

After transferring quickly to a private room, I surrendered to my body's rhythm. My body would decide when to bear down and when to rest, the intensity of labour demanding I be present in my body in a way that I had never known. I had imagined that during childbirth I might be in another place, visiting the spirit world while I birthed my baby. But this was the exact opposite. I was required to be fully and wholly within the present moment and within my body. This experience taught me, profoundly, that the great beyond is not a place far away but viscerally and literally within the body itself.

On my knees with my hands resting on the top of the hospital bed, I looked down at myself and couldn't even recognize the movements I was seeing in my body. My thighs were vibrating with the hum of creation. My body was working so hard to rupture time and space. When Giizik crowned, her head poked out of me calmly for about two minutes. My body relaxed completely and we all revelled in the strange normalcy of the moment. After I pushed a couple more times, she rushed out of me and I held her for the first time. It was 7:24 a.m.—just shy of three hours since

I had first woken up. Giizik was born on a sunny morning at the end of August, just before the crisp fall air rolled into Northwestern Ontario. She weighed six pounds, seven ounces, an early baby who seemed to fall into my lap from the stars.

Blood, water, sweat, and stardust poured out of me the night that I gave birth. As Giizik climbed down the spider's silver thread, all our ancestors gathered in the place before birth to see her off. The low and reverberating moan of creation echoed across the universe to meet mine. The inhalations and exhalations of my ancestors' breath became the rhythm of my body. The pulse of creation rocked my hips back and forth as I flowed with instinctive movement.

The act of giving birth taught me what full and utter wholeness feels like—the ability to be completely present in my body, feeling the swirling smoke inside me travelling up into the sky, being held by my ancestors and the spirits and the totality of expansive creation within a single, fleeting human moment. Each sensation of pain became my guide, an unquestionable tethering of self to body. Each contraction was an invitation to embrace my profound embodiment, calling me back into my body and back into wholeness. My body taught me how to be whole.

As we traversed galaxy and nebula, this being and I each held one end of a rope that bound us together. We used this rope to swing around and around, laughing in playful ecstasy. As we propelled ourselves throughout the starscape, this being began to sing to me, "I have loved you as a mother. I have loved you as a sister. I have loved you as so many things. I will

always come and find you. I will always come and find you to
love you." We howled together in playful laughter, surrounded
by stars. And then I woke up.

If I could imagine many generations ago, so many moons
ago, the sweet and tender embrace between my ancestors
and their children, it would surely resemble the way I hold
my daughter. If I could imagine parenting beyond the grasp
of settler colonialism, beyond the violence and the harm,
I would witness wholeness in its fullest and most embodied form. Parents talk to their children amid the chatter of
spirits who giggle under the weeping moon full of pride.
Children's bodies, relaxed and resourced, traverse their
homelands delighting in the flow of the universe who holds
them softly. I can see the parents surrounded by so many,
constructing the most beautiful web of care for the future.
I can imagine because I see the threads of the past in the
futures we tend to in the here and now.

When I imagine, only one generation ago, my father's
suffering as he was taken to residential school, I feel the
breath pulled from my body. When I imagine, for many
generations, the monstrous grasp of settler colonialism
that distorts our ability to parent, I realize just how hard
the settler colonial project tries to render us incapable
of wholeness. How we raise our children within our web
of relationships is so fundamental to who we are that it
has always been the explicit target of settler colonialism.
Residential schools—places of genocide, torture, and
unimaginable harm—attempted to eradicate Indigenous
children and remove them from our extensive familial and

kinship structures. The usurpation and bastardization of our kinship roles by priests, nuns, and the state harmed children and left parents feeling inadequate, helpless, and full of shame. I can barely bring myself to imagine what it must feel like to have your small child removed from your arms.

My imagination transports me to the present, where I am a parent. It is here where settler colonialism creates the immersive conditions I must parent within. Generations of assaults on our bodies and homelands, on our children and our capacities to show love, bring me to this moment where I still cannot fully comprehend what they did to my father.

Yet I can still glimpse wholeness.

In the soft morning light, my daughter and I tangle ourselves up in the blankets, and when we laugh, our ancestors join us. On a still summer's evening, I watch in awe as my father plays with his granddaughter with the tenderness of everything that could not be taken from him. My daughter runs to hug her great-grandmother and they embrace for endless minutes, a single tear running down my three-year-old's cheek with the deep knowing of what brings us to this moment and the ability to still love.

In the here and now we are broken, but wholeness is a practice, and every day we get closer. I parent through the heaviness, knowing that everything I can give my daughter stands just one generation from the direct assault on our ability to parent, every moment of joy spits in the face of their failed attempts to prevent us from loving, every moment of wholeness in our family is a testament to everything they can never have.

I look at my daughter's sweet and vibrant face in the morning light. The way her firm and round toddler tummy rises and falls with her breath. She looks so peaceful, and I feel like I could explode into one million stars, if only to exist in her gaze forever, in these bodies, and in this time. But my eyes fill with tears because this love has no mercy. Her sweet and delicate face flickers with the faces of the children of Palestine. I am ruptured. She ruptures me and insists that I do not look away. This is the medicine of children. They call us to shape their future.

From the time I was pregnant with Giizik, the love I felt was wholly overwhelming, like a feeling of being reunited, or like a blindfold being taken off to transport me into new dimensions of being and feeling. Every now and then, I feel pangs of sadness when I think about how there will be a time when we will have to leave each other. Every now and then, I sit in quiet disbelief that my time with Giizik as she exists in this physical form is unquestionably fleeting. I revel in the wrinkles on her nose when she smiles. I live in her expression when she looks out the car window deep in thought. Although I know we have loved each other in different forms before, and will find each other again, there is an anticipatory grief around the loss of loving each other in these specific bodies during this specific time. When I feel the depth of this love, and the grief I am so privileged to only anticipate, I think of the children of Palestine. It is such a profound loss to be robbed of loving your child in the here and now, even with the potential for reunion. Giizik teaches me to remember the depth of injustice, and my body remembers the pain of genocide.

I have come to understand parenting as a form of creative practice. Anishinaabe creative practice is the responsibility to build our world in collaboration with all the relationships that make us whole—the ability to dance wildly within our web of creation in order to build futures of justice and goodness. For us, creative practice is not bound to the art world or the creation of artworks, but rather it is an expansive practice of worldbuilding that involves accessing the full scope of our relationality that traverses from earth to sky. From this understanding, creative practice encompasses parenting.

Anishinaabe parenting, to touch the future every day through my daughter. Anishinaabe parenting, to dream and enact the worlds that will better hold all our children. In acknowledging Anishinaabe parenting as creative practice, I am crediting the love and labour that extends to me from the great beyond, I am honouring the knowledge that lives in my own body, and I am standing firm in my responsibility to shape a more just and liberatory future for us all.

Anishinaabe creative practice involves both the act of dreaming and the act of doing. The act of dreaming requires us to envision and imagine better worlds that are informed by both the witnessing of our current reality and the gathering of knowledge from all our relationships. With art, sometimes the dreaming can be the moments when paint is spilled across canvas to mark our world, the artwork itself, or the reflection surrounding the work.

With parenting, I have found that the dreaming takes place during moments of stillness, the moments when we are offered space for deep reflection with bodies that are activated in different ways. When I was pregnant, I was in a constant state of dreaming while the great beyond swirled within my belly. After Giizik was born, feeding her from my body became a creative space of dreaming. Sitting in stillness for hours, I would get lost in her never-ending eyes, dreaming of worlds outside of the mess of settler colonialism. Now, I am prompted to access moments of stillness by my daughter herself—when she demands that I am present, when I am cooking for her, or when I am putting her to bed, lying in the dark with her steady breath beside me. The activations of our bodies happen in myriad ways, and are in no way limited to carrying or feeding a child, but parenting asks us to dream up new futures in conversation with the brilliance of our bodies.

The other part of creative practice, the act of doing, is ensuring that the worlds we dream become material reality. With art, this can mean extending the impact of my art to my community in tangible ways. With parenting, the act of doing is inherently built into the practice itself. Every decision we make, every word we speak, directly shapes the future contained within the bodies of our children. Every dream we choose to make real, or to ignore, is how we build our world, whether we choose to orient ourselves toward this reality or not. Unlike art, which is often compartmentalized in the settler colonial context to be solely about the act of dreaming at the expense of material contributions to our communities and homelands, participating in a practice of worldbuilding is absolutely inevitable for the parent. In the opposite fashion, parenting is often compartmentalized to be about the act of doing rather than the act of dreaming.

However creative practice is compartmentalized within the logics of settler colonialism, it is meant to prevent us from understanding our responsibilities and capabilities to impact, shape, and change our world. In the settler colonial world, art and parenting are rendered apolitical through these compartmentalizations. They do everything they can to prevent our art from becoming reality and our children from ushering in new worlds.

In the settler colonial world, parenting becomes about doing and not about dreaming. This separation of dreaming from doing removes our ability to think about parenting as a practice of worldbuilding. We are no longer required to bear witness to the world around us in order to transcend its harm. We are no longer required to dream with our whole bodies and access the love and care of our ancestors and spirit kin to help us build a better world. We are only required to uncritically do, and the act of doing is truncated to be about a child's physical, mental, and emotional needs.

In a broad sense, within the confines of the Western world, parents do not dream futures for their children outside the parameters already set by the infrastructure of settler colonialism. Within the confines of the Western world, parents are encouraged to claim no responsibility for their contributions to the larger world that supports their child, only for the health and wellness of the child alone. Within the confines of the Western world, parenting as an expansive dance with all our relations in order to craft a beautiful future is relegated to a sanitized, truncated, and limited responsibility to keep an individual child well and on a trajectory to accept the colonial conditions around them.

Entire generations do not believe they have a responsibility or the ability to change the world around them—an insidious mechanism to prevent resistance to, and transcendence from, the clutches of settler colonialism.

Obscuring our ability and duty to worldbuild stands as one of the most insidious strategies for settler colonialism to hegemonize itself. I saw this most overtly in the fall of 2023, in the thick of the escalated genocide in Palestine, when I watched parents confront the self-maintained limits of their ability to influence the world around them. Within the imperial core, parents who were enraged and distraught about the genocide found nowhere else to go beyond these emotions: *I'm so sad, but how am I supposed to change anything? I'm so angry, but nothing I can do will stop what is happening. I need to take a step back from the news because I have my own children to care for.* These sentiments existed on a spectrum. On one end, many simply used these admonitions to absolve themselves of the guilt of doing nothing and to avoid acknowledging that they actively consent to a world built on genocide. On the other end of the spectrum, where people were really struggling and trying to move into a place of action, they would come up against a sort of ontological confinement in which they could not possibly understand that they have the ability to influence the world around them. They could not possibly fathom that, whether they can see it or not, every moment of every day, consisting of both action and inaction, contributes to the building of our world.

In the West, many parents are conditioned to remove themselves entirely from the processes of worldbuilding.

This conditioning happens first through the axes of privilege that are sustained and governed by the colonial project. If you experience enough privilege in your life, why would you want to change the world around you? Many parents exist in a world already built for them, such that, when a time comes when they do want to change the world, they doubt their ability to even make an impact.

On the contrary, folks who bear the brunt of the oppression that makes the privilege of others possible are by necessity engaged in processes of worldbuilding every single day in order to survive. For many Indigenous and racialized folks, worldbuilding is both a practical necessity for survival and an inherent part of our worldviews and ways of being. The fall of 2023 illuminated the architecture of settler colonial normalization. Even those who were shaken within the protection of their privilege to move to action were so far removed from the practice of worldbuilding that they remained languishing in inaction. We cannot take this illumination for granted, and we must work to reclaim our ability and responsibility to build our world, every single moment of every single day.

When we brought Palestinian organizers from the Toronto region to Treaty 3 homelands, we were forging a pathway to our collective wholeness. The skies parted and the thunderbirds celebrated our arrival. The land shook with the love and rage of all our ancestors. Giizik prayed for the bears and the water in the bush before uplifting us with the sacred silliness of a toddler. There was so much goodness—yet the bombing never stopped. How could something be so monumental yet unable to stop the harm? Hope is a practice of worldbuilding. Every embrace, every shared meal, every sob an invocation for a future of wholeness. Every moment spent together an invocation for a future of wholeness. The ripples travel across the sea undetected like soft wind on water, but they will reach Falasteen.

Settler colonialism is a complex matrix of power that is organized through its rampant compartmentalizations that separate, distinguish, and create systems of value for hierarchy and domination. These compartmentalizations extend to the realm of parenting and are multi-dimensional and complex. From the compartmentalization of parent from child to the separation of parent from their web of extended kinship, parenting becomes a sterilized and diminished practice within the settler colonial world. Even the term *parenting* denotes the heteronormative birth parents of a child rather than acknowledging the expanse of people who contribute to the raising of a child. When a baby is born, there is too much power and connection between the child and their web of care that threatens the fragile fabric of settler colonialism. When a baby is birthed from a body, there is too much potential for people to remember their ancestors and the hum of everything they need within themselves. When a child is growing, there is too much medicine in the ways they bring people together and allow us all to revel in futures informed from the great beyond. Our ability to parent in fullness and in its entirety must be diminished for settler colonialism to have even a hope to rule.

One of the very first compartmentalizations to surround

a child is the construction of parenthood as synonymous with the nuclear family, or the separation of parents and children from their extended structures of kinship and care. Children are born into families that are already individualized from the broader community. The nuclear family, which consists of the cisheteropatriarchal pairing of mother and father to create child, is the unit of capitalism, and the nuclear family is privileged at the expense of other ways of organizing ourselves. Parents are separated from the aunties, uncles, grandparents, and community folk who would traditionally take on various dimensions of parental responsibility. The responsibility to parent a child is solely placed on the shoulders of the mother and father. This tactic of colonialism serves to under-resource parents so that they are unable to even consider their larger responsibilities of worldbuilding, while also severing the intimacy and connection between the nuclear family and its web of relationality. The less we can rely on our community, the more we are forced to rely on capitalism and the structures of settler colonialism to fulfill our needs.

From an Anishinaabe understanding of parenting as creative practice, many people contribute to the practice of parenting. Just like the fluidity of a rushing river, primary and secondary responsibilities to a child shift and flow, mingling with everyone's inherent responsibility to build a better and more just world for us all. The ways in which we organize our kinship structures are varied and diverse, spilling over the rigidity of the nuclear family. The biological essentialism of the nuclear family that not only privileges cisgender and heteronormative couples but also restricts motherhood and fatherhood to blood, DNA, and body is a colonial construct that has no place in our communities. We can parent children who didn't come from our bodies with the same intimacy and interconnectedness. We can dance with our children in the great beyond through our bodies despite our biological relationship to them. Our bodies are so complex that they evade the containerizations of motherhood and fatherhood as the primary identities from which to parent. And so, when I talk about being a parent, I am referencing the more expansive exploration of a term that includes everyone who contributes to the spectrum of parenting. And when I talk about doing so through our bodies, it is not limited to carrying a child or body feeding, but rather encompasses our ability to access our ancestors and the great beyond through the medicine of children.

The next colonial compartmentalization is child from parent, which is the genesis and sustainer of individualism. Beginning at childbirth, parents are encouraged, coerced, and forced to establish degrees of separation between themselves and their children. Not long ago, the standard practice in Western health care was to immediately remove babies from their birthing parent, and parents were encouraged en masse to feed their babies with formula as a safer and easier option than body feeding. As their children enter toddlerhood, parents navigate the pressure to sleep train them so that they can sleep separately and put them into daycares as they confront the impossibility of child rearing while having to make a living. None of these decisions made as an informed choice reflect a lacking parent in any way, but the forceful imposition of these practices by the settler colonial state constitutes a strategy to separate child from parent. From birth, even with a small and new being, individualism must be established, and the parent must remain oriented around their own individual participation in the structures of settler colonialism, the genesis of individualism.

When Giizik was born, I was lucky to have midwives who advocated that she be kept in my arms from the moment I gave birth. She was so warm and familiar, and for the first six months, she barely left my arms. My perspective at that time was that we were still sharing a body. Having just come from the stars and the swirling sky of our ancestors, she would naturally need a transition period for her to land in her own body, and she would need to lean on mine. I fed Giizik from my body for two years and eight months, but our decision to body feed was but one singular way of so many that we shared our bodies. Sharing a body is not confined to the literal and physical ways we can choose to share our body to support a small child. When I say sharing a body, it is important to remember that the body is not limited to the physical, but also includes ancestors, homelands, and the great beyond. Sharing a body also means revelling in each other's orbits and delighting in the sweetness of creation together. Sharing a body means feeling the constellations between us flicker when we are skin to skin. Sharing a body means becoming whole through the impartial fullness of one another.

During Giizik's early life, feeding her from my body became one of the most challenging, intimate, and transcendent experiences that allowed me to understand parenting as creative practice. The pressures that surround the topic of body feeding are contradictory. Not very long ago, the practice was actively discouraged by medical professionals. Today, there is a movement wherein people are shamed if they choose not to body feed. And yet even if you do body feed, you should do it in secrecy and only for a short amount of time, or else you are inappropriate. Despite these pressures, the decision to feed Giizik from my body was the one that worked best for our relationship. When I fed Giizik from my body, it was like we became a portal to the great beyond. Her body, birthed not only from mine but from the cosmic sweetness of all that we are, allowed me to glimpse the galaxies we come from and feel whole. For hours, I would sit in my rocking chair dreaming of worlds that I would paint and live out years later. For hours, I would bathe in her peaceful gaze of absolute safety and ease. Body feeding became a space for creative practice, and the act of dreaming new worlds for all of us that I could then put into motion through the act of parenting.

As I was body feeding, I was also deeply emotional. Western medicine attributes this change in emotions solely to the shifting hormones in the body. Although my hormones were certainly changing, I felt like my emotional changes were more connected to my new-found ability to touch the great beyond through my daughter. Body feeding allowed me to spend more visceral time with my ancestors and feel the pulse of the universe flow out of me like a cosmic river. Body feeding cultivated a sacred empathy within me, in which my lived reality was now more tethered to the greater dimensions of love and care that extend to us from beyond this world. This deepened empathy and compassion made me care even more about all living beings around me, and sharpened my dedication to a more radical practice of worldbuilding. Witnessing any form of pain and suffering around me now moved me more deeply than it ever had before. Importantly, this sacred empathy wasn't a fleeting hormonal change in my body, but a permanent evolution that continues to root me in a greater sense of responsibility to build a better future.

Oh, the sweetness of your eyes. You look up at me with adoration, and your eyes sparkle with the radiance of a future so bright it takes my breath away. Oh, to glimpse the future through your focused gaze as I feed you. The infant with his eyes wide open, who was killed at his mother's chest with those same eyes of adoration and future, also takes my breath away. I saw his eyes only after he was gone, an unjust ending of one future that must, by all laws of everything good and whole, spark a new one in me. That sacred empathy, my daughter lying quietly beside me in rest, my eyes close as I take a breath. I move beyond sadness and beyond grief, my body held in place by my commitment to build a world where babies remain our futures unfolded.

As Giizik grew older and entered the era of tantrums and meltdowns, my Anishinaabe worldview continued to conceptualize us as a collaborative unit rather than two individuals on a quest for independence within colonial society. If she was having a tough time, I needed to help our unit. If we had to leave a place I had really wanted to be in, there was no room for resentment because I was not separate from Giizik. It was simply a reality that we both had to move through. With this shift in thinking, a child, even in their most difficult hour, is not a burden or impediment, because they are an inherent part of their parent, a part that needs more love and care for a very short period of time in the grand scheme of things.

During Giizik's toddler years, we shared a body. Again, not just in a physical sense; beyond pregnancy and beyond body feeding, we shared a body in that we shared an orbit within our intimate webs of creation. We needed to be close during this time to learn from one another. From me, she learns how to care for herself and how to become independent, not within settler colonial society but within her sense of responsibility and role in the world. From her, I learn how to better tend to the futures we need, and I am able to touch the great beyond every day through her sparkling eyes.

A successful parent in the Western world has established independence from their child such that they do not falter in their contributions to capitalism. During Giizik's early life, I encountered the pressure to strive for the kind of independence that is at the heart of individualism. Parents cannot escape the expectation to strive for the independence required to remain firmly rooted in individualism. *Is she sleeping through the night? Is she in her crib yet? When will you go back to work? When will you stop body feeding?* Overlaid on these incessant questions to assess independence are projections of shame and judgment. If she is sleeping through the night, I ought to be ashamed that she is doing so through co-sleeping. If I'm back at work, it is too early, and if I'm not, I am a failure. If I choose to body feed for the first six months, that's amazing, but more than two years is disgusting. A parent cannot win, and this is exactly the point. These layers of shame and judgment are mechanisms of settler colonialism that attempt to keep parents locked within a cycle of external validation and control. Parents are forced to question every decision and look outside themselves for the right answers, rather than inward toward their own bodies, knowledge, and communities.

Sometimes, but not always, parenting my daughter feels so effortless. There are things deep inside of me, tucked away in bone and belly, that have been taken care of for generations by the delicate dance of ancestor within body. When I gave birth, I felt it so strongly. I knew exactly what to do. As I parent, I feel it too. We have everything we need within our bodies to parent our children.

The settler colonial compartmentalizations of parenting are bolstered and influenced by the overarching structure of ageism. Through ageism, adults who can work are privileged at the expense of children and Elders, who are deemed inferior because of their lack of contributions to capitalism. As well, ableism must posit children as inherently dumb, menial, and "blank-state" beings such that parents can assume complete power over their child to determine all aspects of their life, forwarding a parenting approach that is rooted in paternalism, domination, and hierarchy. Here, the idea of a child as a burden becomes deeply rooted throughout settler society. Beginning with the constructed inferiority of a child through the structure of ageism, any struggle within parenting can now be blamed on the child, generating resentment and distance between child and parent. The notion of children as a burden reinforces the individualism that settler colonialism requires. Children become impediments to our independence, and the impetus for getting them to behave within colonial society becomes greater.

Within the structures of ageism and capitalism, parents become the ultimate conditioners and practitioners of settler colonialism, mimicking the domination of colonialism itself in order to control their children, proclaiming: *I will teach you how to live in this settler colonial world, but not how to transcend it or even question it.* A child's obedience becomes the marker of a good parent and provides the independence necessary for the parent to contribute to capitalism. Although children do need help learning the curvature of this earth, the settler colonial world refuses to acknowledge that they may have their own internal knowledge and gifts, and the knowledge transfer remains unilateral and hierarchical. I often wonder if children's expressions of silliness and unruliness are uncomfortable reminders to adults of their lack of freedom and wholeness within the settler colonial world. In a public place, seeing a child singing at the top of their lungs, bending their limbs into a pretzel without a care in the world, or thrashing their body in unfiltered rage can garner dirty looks or comments that the parent better discipline their child. Adults find the sight of children being free repulsive and inappropriate because those are easier emotions than the ones that lead us to materially challenge our own conditions of non-freedom.

In a society where children are seen as inferior impediments to our ability to live an independent and productive life, children must also be compartmentalized from larger society. There is an entire industry of child-specific spaces that subtly create the distinctions of where children should and should not be. To be clear, the problem isn't that these spaces exist, but rather that there is an expectation for parents to mostly orient themselves around these child-friendly spaces such that children are compartmentalized away from other areas of our lives. Parents experience the pressure to do so through the microaggressions they face when bringing children into various non-child spaces. They also experience this pressure through the structure of ageism, which infantilizes children and provides the justification to keep children within developmentally stimulating and age-appropriate environments. Lastly, they experience this pressure through the compartmentalization of parenting that relegates their responsibilities to keeping a child safe, fed, and developmentally well. These child-friendly places become a way to evade the discomfort of having children in a society that loathes children, and also serve as a marker of a good parent in a society that only values a child's basic and developmental needs.

Since Giizik was born, I have felt bombarded with people's projections of children as a burden and of parenting as a practice of suffering. Parents seek support by sharing their experiences, but whenever I share mine in a way that doesn't present my child as a burden or my experience as one of suffering, I am met by assurances that one day things will change. The rhetoric of "just you wait" colours the ways in which parents have tried to connect with me—*You're never going to sleep again. You're never going to be yourself again. Kiss your life goodbye.* These sentiments are everywhere.

Many of the parents around me seem to compartmentalize themselves into discrete parenting identities. Rather than connecting as full human beings, parents I encounter through Giizik's school or camps want only to talk about the minutiae of parenting, and only within child-friendly places: *I can't go there, I am a parent now. I can't be that anymore, I am a parent now.* I have found myself unable to relate to many peripheral parents around me who seem to have committed to the compartmentalizations of parenting within the confines of settler colonialism. Although parenting can absolutely be a process of suffering, these projections feel like a way to normalize the idea of children as a burden. Although parenting can be all-consuming, reducing parents to that role alone is a way to normalize the idea that parenting should be apolitical. Apolitical parenting denies the broader responsibilities all caregivers have to materially transform the world into a more just, whole, and safe place for all children.

Since October 2023, even the ground I stand on feels unstable. I looked down at my phone, checking the updates from Palestine during the sixty-minute window I had while Giizik was in her dance class. In that moment, I could not bear the chatter of other parents around me. The building of a new school that will change the neighbourhood. Vacation plans for the upcoming summer. The latest water bottle for children. Their bedtime routines. We spent an hour together

every week, and this must have been at least the twenti-
eth week, and this was always the conversation. That day I
couldn't take it. I wept in the bathroom.

Yet another compartmentalization of parenting is the separation of parent from the larger expanse of their human-ity. As a parent, we are first and foremost removed from our larger structures of kinship and community care to support the parenting of a child. Furthermore, parents are told they have no internal knowledge or resources and must look for external information on how to be a parent. The obscuring of a parent's internal resources is a product of the complex structures of settler colonialism that remove body from homelands, ancestors, and the greater web of creation. This isolation of the parent from their larger community necessitates external learning that can now be bound and shaped by settler colonialism. There is a whole educational industry devoted to parenting, from dealing with toddler tantrums to sleep training a child.

Although we do need external help sometimes, the norm for Western parents has been to rely on disembodied infor-mation that excludes the political dimensions of parenting that demand we are responsible for building a better world. Parents are told that they must only keep a child fed, well, and stimulated in order to be good parents. Parents are actively discouraged from feeling like they have the love of their ancestors within their own bodies helping them to care for their children. Parents are actively discouraged from feeling like they have the tools they need within their bones to raise children in a world better than this one.

All these complex compartmentalizations—child from parent, child from society, parent from extended care, the act of dreaming from the responsibility of worldbuilding—cultivate the Western framework for parenting that relies on authority, domination, and hierarchy. Within this framework, parenting is compartmentalized to be solely about control and obedience, health and wellness, removing the parent from their responsibility to build a more just world for all children. Ultimately, this framework primes children for a life of obedience within settler colonial power structures and prevents everyone involved from resourcing themselves through their bodies, their ancestors, and their web of creation.

In this world, children grow into adults who believe they are worthless unless they are contributing to capitalism. In this world, parents also feel worthless outside their ability to control and dominate their children, while maintaining their own participation in capitalism. It is a cold and dark world of immense harm and hurt for everyone.

When I was pregnant, I was standing on the precipice of a huge unknown, unsure of what type of parent I would be. I knew that I was birthed into a settler colonial world of harm. I knew that I came from such targeted attacks on our sense of kinship and also on our bodies. But from the moment Giizik was born, I felt an effortlessly innate ability to parent my daughter. It didn't necessarily require my labour but rather the labour and love emanating to me from my ancestors. And it was inside me, inside my body. All this beautiful knowledge swirled inside my belly when I was pregnant and spilled out of me with blood when she was born.

Of course, there have been many times when parenting has been hard. But throughout my journey of becoming a parent, there have also been many times when I have felt so resourced through the great beyond that my daughter and I are swimming through. This is something that is simply not acknowledged within mainstream parenting narratives. We have everything we need within our bodies. Our ancestors are waiting for us to listen to their knowledge.

Parenting as creative practice is what allows me to glimpse wholeness. Through parenting, I am able to dance with all my ancestors in the great beyond who teach me how to shape the world alongside my daughter. Through the eyes of my daughter, I glimpse past, present, and future, learning how to paint our world with splashes of creation that come from the place beyond time. Parenting requires me to be present within my body, even if that presence isn't absolute. My body, my daughter's body, and the bodies of all my ancestors weave together in moments of sacred stillness so we can bathe in our wholeness. Although parenting is laborious and challenging in the settler colonial world, my body can never be compartmentalized when it is flickering with the starlight of the constellations my daughter came from.

Giizik, you are a worldbuilder. Before you turned one, you instilled a wave of courage in me to make things right with my own mother. In one flash of your gummy smile, you closed years of distance between us.

Before you turned two, you rearranged my life, bringing so many people closer to us with the medicine of who you are.

Just after you turned three, you stood beside me so strong while I wailed and contorted my body as I witnessed the genocide of the people of Palestine. You took my head in your hands and asked me if my heart was breaking.

Before you turned four, you orchestrated a world of Palestinians and Anishinaabeg working together, and you danced with all of us on our proud homelands. Saying your prayer at the foot of a tall birch tree, you spoke of Palestine and mukwa, love and spirits.

Sometimes, when you are playing, I can hear you say, "Gaza, Gaza, don't you cry. Palestine will never die." Sometimes, you seem to know what people need with the wisdom of an Elder. There is a deep knowing in your eyes of what you came here to do and what you have already seen when you sat in the stars, reflected in what I am able to give. But most of all, I know your knowledge and brilliance through what you have changed in me.

If I could imagine, many generations, many moons ago, the boundless joy of my ancestors as children, I would surely glimpse that same look of wholeness that is contained in my daughter's gaze. If I could imagine, beyond the compartmentalizations of settler colonialism, the flickering of our children's bodies between earth, water, star, and sky, it would be enough for us to transcend this mess. My imagination brings me to the present, where I glimpse wholeness every day through my daughter. I witness her inherent wholeness and I am reminded of the medicine of all children.

The children, whole beings who are connected so intimately to creation, innocent in their intrinsic wholeness, carriers of medicine for the future we must fight for. The children, whose wholeness makes them the target of settler colonial violence, for they are so very threatening when they bring a piece of the great beyond to us all.

I lie in bed beside my daughter and weep for the children of Palestine. The whole and full children of Palestine who bear the brunt of a relentless genocide. My daughter has taught me so much about what it means to build a better world. She has demanded, with my body and hers, that I tend to a future free of genocide, a future where children live out their wholeness as they become adults, dancing with all that they are.

Through my daughter, I fight harder for my wholeness. Through my body, I am taught a pathway to the swirling smoke inside me. Through parenting, I become full and whole.

Chapter 7

On Wholeness and Feeling Good
*Embodied pleasure and the intergenerational
reclamation of bodies full and whole*

*What I wouldn't give to travel back in time and embrace my
ancestors as children. I would hold them in my arms and
fill them with the love and certainty of futures embodied.
What I wouldn't give to bestow my homelands with utter
joy, at the moment they were flooded and could not recognize themselves. All the while, they do the same for me. The
waters of my homelands contained within my body beg me to
be whole. My ancestors gather at the edge of my skin to pray
for my fullness and the ability to feel deserving and worthy
of pleasure in this life.*

To live in an Indigenous body is to materially and
symbolically be harmed and hated. Settler colonialism has
worked very hard to make it so. For generations, our bodies
have endured relentless forms of violence that permeate the
fabric of our being. If we can survive the genocidal conditions around us, we still live with the rippling impact of
this violence on our bodies that is layered, complex, and
entangled. Among its many strategies, settler colonialism

has explicitly targeted our capacity to feel pleasure in our bodies as a mechanism of genocide and a disconnection of spirit from body. Many of us find ourselves with a diminished capacity to be present in our bodies and struggle with feeling worthy and deserving of pleasure and wholeness. Attempting to remove us from our ability to feel pleasure is deeply political—a means to remove self from body in order to make it easier to materially remove our bodies from our homelands. When we are present in our bodies, filled with desire to dance with everything that we are and welcoming to our wholeness, we are deeply threatening to the settler colonial project. When we are able to feel pleasure, we are convening with our ancestors, spirits, and the great beyond in ways that make us incomprehensibly resistant to the settler colonial state.

Anishinaabe pleasure is the practice of feeling whole in bodies harmed and hated. Anishinaabe pleasure is communing with everything inside our body—the stars, the muskrat, and the moist earth that smells of rain. Pleasure is more than just the physical; it is to be whole beyond body and time. Pleasure is more than just a sensation; it is a reminder of the euphoria of our existence while we convene with everything we are beyond this specific body. Pleasure is like dancing with your own mortality—gazing at your specific body in the here and now and saying, "I choose you, and I choose to revel in your sweetness that is always fleeting. I choose to feel good. Despite the harm, despite the violence, I choose to feel good." Pleasure is the low moan of creation shaking itself out of slumber, ready to rupture with fullness.

Pleasure exists in many forms but is always rooted in the body. While our bodies can feel whole in many different ways, pleasure demands desire as the prerequisite to our wholeness. We must want to receive it, and behind this want is the ability to feel deserving and worthy of wholeness in our bodies, a practice so many of us struggle with in the colonial context.

As Anishinaabe people, we do not limit our bodies to the physical and they also contain the smoke of the great beyond. Under our skin, our ancestors swirl with the movement of our breath; the waters of our homelands flow in our tears; and we exhale the stardust we come from. To feel pleasure in these bodies is to restore our wholeness and dance in joy and reverence with all that we are. Here, I will mostly focus on pleasure within the context of sex because this is where I have been affected most deeply by settler colonialism. Importantly, when I reference pleasure in relationship to sex, I am foregrounding the struggle to experience pleasure even within myself and the ways in which settler colonialism has impacted the intimacy I have between myself and my body. It is important to remember that pleasure exists outside of these limited dimensions of sex and cannot be so easily compartmentalized. Pleasure binds the physical body to its larger dimensions, demanding that we intimately convene with both the expanse of the universe outside of us and within our own specific bodies, even though these bodies might be hurting from our immersion in colonial violence. Pleasure is the methodology to make wholeness last for more than a fleeting moment; it is the ability to wake up every day and centre our desire to be whole and to feel good in our bodies. Pleasure is all the ways we experience good sensations in our bodies, not limited by sex or touch, in conjunction with all the relations that make us whole.

Breath fills me with the same rocking rhythm of creation. The night is still and heavy with the voices of busy spirits travelling the skies, electric. When I cannot bear to look at myself, my body stirs with whispers of desire to call me home. When I do not want to touch myself, the bears surround me and tell me that they love me, infinitely and without question. When I do not want to feel, the water comes from inside me to wash the pain away. Our pleasure is not just our own because we are never alone.

It is hard for me to imagine the boundless forms of pleasure my ancient ancestors experienced in their bodies because my imagination is stifled by my own experiences of harm. These experiences of harm cut across the expanse of what it means to be a human being, creating the confines of an imaginary limited by loss and violence, supported by shame and harm. Particularly when harm happens to young bodies, these imaginary confines can restructure reality to create new material truths. Stated differently, settler colonialism has been so immersive for so long that I feel like I have been robbed of my vision of what pleasure could look like for my ancestors, for my family, and for myself.

My work now is to deconstruct my own confinement in order to see the incalculable potential around me for Anishinaabe wholeness in our bodies. I sit with myself and look at my body. With each deep breath, my body teaches me how to imagine wholeness so that I may dream it into reality.

My body, I will sit with you.

My body, I will get to know you.

It is what we deserve.

The pulsing breath of creation. The guttural grunting of bears foraging in the bush. The chatter of frogs as the sun sets over the lake. The sound of my own breath quickening. I run my hands up my thigh, lingering on the marked bears who guard my wholeness, and I close my eyes. My legs birth a river that trickles onto the bed. My homelands quiver in delight and my ancestors chuckle with joy. Our pleasure has always made us whole.

One of the foundational strategies of settler colonialism has always been, and continues to be, sexual violence. Since contact, the bodies of certain people in our communities have been branded as disposable and open for conquest in order to encourage mass sexual violence. Just like our homelands were represented as vacant and empty lands for the taking, so too were the bodies of Indigenous women, Two-Spirit, trans, and queer people in our communities. Sexual violence toward Indigenous people was sanctioned by the state and contained in the values and ideals of early settler colonialism that continue to this day. This country continues to be founded on the trespass of Indigenous bodies, from Native women being forced to trade their bodies in order to gain permission to leave their reserves from the Indian Agent to the unfathomable number of missing and murdered Indigenous women, girls, Two-Spirit, and trans people. They continue to target the people in our communities who hold the most power, who stitch the constellations on our bodies and remind us of everything we are.

While the early settler state used strategies of genocide and erasure to contest the existence of those outside of the constructed gender binary, Indigenous women faced, and continue to experience, a specific set of public-facing harmful representations. In the settler colonial world, Indigenous women are represented as licentious, dirty, and inferior. The goal is to dehumanize us enough to encourage the harm and conquest of our bodies that is central to the continued existence of the settler state. Although these strategies are obscured in the neocolonial context of today, they continue in more insidious ways. In courtrooms, our killers are never punished. In landfills, our remains are never recovered. On our homelands, our lives continue to end due to violence.

To be an Indigenous woman is to live in a body harmed and hated. To be an Indigenous woman is to contend often with the possibility of dying through violence. To birth an Indigenous daughter is to wail into the empty night at what she has inherited.

I want to be whole, if not for me then for you, Giizik. I want you to look at your mother and see her radiating fullness and delight in her own existence and body, despite the harmful conditions we continue to face. I want you to be whole, not for anyone but yourself. I want, so badly, for the stories of harm to become so distant that they are only a whisper and not a threat that we think of every single day.

As settler colonialism established itself by the trespassing of Indigenous lands and bodies, it clarified its attacks on our relationships to pleasure and the body. Across Turtle Island, residential schools systematically violated and assaulted the bodies of Indigenous children through barbaric sexual violence. While the focus of residential schools is often seen through a lens of attempted assimilation and removing children from their families, so many of these schools employed sustained, intentional, and systematic sexual violence that demonstrates the centrality of this tactic to colonial settlement and occupation.

At St. Margaret's residential school in Fort Frances, my father was raped and assaulted regularly from the age of seven to sixteen by multiple priests and nuns working at the school. His story is not unique, though his ability to be so open about it is uncommon. The scale of this sexual abuse, coupled with the torture, starvation, and cruelty of the residential school system, robbed generations of Indigenous peoples of their sense of self, body, pleasure, and love. Residential schools made the body of the child so uninhabitable that they could not bear to live in its presence. Many children died in the schools because of neglect, medical experimentation, and outright violence. Many children grew up to take their own lives after what had happened to their bodies. If they survived to become an adult, many struggled to feel or understand love and grappled with distorted relationships to pleasure, their body, and the bodies of others.

In the era of reconciliation, the state ensures that the focus of public dialogue remains oriented around healing our people in relation to forced assimilation, forwarding a sanitized narrative that obscures these more sinister harms. In classrooms across the country, students learn that residential schools are a sad chapter in history, an honest mistake of trying to teach the Indian how to live in the new world. Public discourse avoids talking about how the Canadian state intentionally stole generations of small children from their homes to systematically rape and torture them, conducting hunger and human-limit experiments fuelled by the emptiness of their un-belonging on these lands. The realities of the residential school system reveal what settler colonialism deems threatening enough to attack with severe force and horror. Our pleasure and wholeness make them tremble in fear. Our bodies have always terrified them.

When I trace Anishinaabe relationships to pleasure inter-generationally, their distortion begins and ends with settler colonialism. For my ancestors who existed before colonialism, pleasure was an inherent right and a fact of life. For these ancestors, life was not perfect, but they were certainly present in their bodies, whole and full like the moon who cares for them. I have heard stories of ancestors in my family who had as many partners as the stars in the piece of sky that birthed them. I have heard fragmented stories of love, heartbreak, loss, and companionship. But mostly, our stories about our pleasure and joy are quiet stories.

I like to imagine that my great-grandparents loved each other fiercely and boundlessly, shaking the earth with their collective wholeness and reprieve in each other as they weathered the colonial storm. I like to imagine that my father, until the age of seven, was held by this same love that taught him his body was beautiful and brown and wild and flickering.

I am forced to imagine the depth of utter loss and pain when my father was taken from his mother and his grandparents who were helping to raise him and forced to go to residential school. I am forced to confront the endless despair and anguish of these loving caregivers coming to understand that his small body was subjected to such cruel and horrific sexual abuse and torture. And I do not have to imagine the stories of this abuse and torture. These are the stories we live with and must carry. These are the stories we tell. In some families, these stories are quiet whispers. But in mine, they have always been loud. My father's insistence on us understanding this injustice is an invocation for our wholeness.

Settler colonialism not only harms us but also uses shame as a tool to obscure the source of that harm. In the confines of shame, we are unable to see harm as external and systemic, instead directing our resentment toward our own bodies, families, and communities. We live quietly in our experiences of pleasure, or lack thereof. We live quietly in our experiences of harm and the trespassing of our bodies. Most of us continue to live quietly in the wreckage of our communities from the residential school system, wading through dimensions of distorted love and pleasure that are so complexly fragmented precisely because that was the intention. Not just the rape and assault of children, but also forcing them to harm each other, forcing them to harm animals. Not just the sustained abuse of children, but also making them help bury murdered babies, making them bury their friends. Not just the violence of the school itself, but also the pain of running away from the school only to be returned by the community. Not just the violence toward the children, but also the mechanisms to keep their families in fear, the twisted ways it was ensured that there truly was no way to escape. Not just the hunger experiments, but also beating children into submission while telling them they are disgusting and worthless.

Amid all this unspeakable violence, carried across so many generations since contact, it is easier to forgo our desire for wholeness than it is to acknowledge how our ability to feel pleasure has been taken from us. We convince ourselves that pleasure, the ability to feel good and be present in our bodies, is not what we want or need. In our shame that is orchestrated by the hands of the settler colonial machine, we live with the echoes of colonial violence and residential school—intense disassociation from our bodies, associations of pleasure with harm and violence, deeply rooted internalizations of the Indigenous body as dirty and worthless, the notion of sex and pleasure as something unspeakable. It becomes safer to exist within the settler colonial imaginary of pleasure, wherein it is relegated to frivolity and the strictly physical, than it is to remember that pleasure is our inherent wholeness that ripples to our ancestors and the great beyond.

For all these reasons, pleasure and sex is still a taboo topic for our communities, one we often avoid because of its nuanced and traumatic layers. It can be deeply triggering to the generations who have experienced such enormous violations of body and pleasure. It can be deeply triggering to those who have had distorted Christian beliefs quite literally beaten into them—that the Indigenous body is not human, that sex is sin, that our culture is demonic and evil. And so, the stories about our bodies, in the here and now, are usually quiet. Many of us have been gravely disembodied from our desire to feel pleasure and worthiness in our bodies, the type of pleasure that weaves our bodies into the constellations we come from.

My ancestors whispered to me in the night. I was twenty-four at the time, and they blew stardust across my body as I slept. When I woke up, I had a desire to paint my body. I had a desire to paint my body feeling pleasure under the watchful moon. With the bears who love me so, with the ancestors who pour out of my wholeness, with the blood of my body, and the blood of all my ancestors whose bodies have been violated, I painted my own invocation for wholeness.

The intergenerational weight of such unimaginable bodily harm bears down heavily on my body. I think I have inherited a certain degree of protective numbness, and I will spend my life fighting to become more present in my body again, but I still glimpse wholeness. As someone who did not grow up on a reserve because of our collective displacement, and as someone who has a close proximity to whiteness through my mother, I have grappled largely with forms of harm that emanate from the urban

Indigenous experience—the confrontation of Indigenous self with the largely non-Indigenous world. My experiences of bodily harm emerge from the broader dehumanization of Indigenous women that submerges my body in a thick bog made of heavy sludge and debris where it is so hard to move. In this bog, Native women are dirty and inferior yet also hypersexualized and asking for it.

Sometimes, the relentless sexual gaze of white men presents to me as an ontological conundrum of the settler desire to belong. They must see me as an object to be conquered because it allows them to justify how they have constructed their own belonging on these stolen lands. If they see me as a human being, they must confront their own immorality.

Sometimes, the unending fetishization of my body presents to me as a necessity within the process of othering Indigenous people. I must be viewed as an exotic artifact so that I am the foreign one in the equation, an othering both in terms of place and humanity. Always, the attempted and at times successful trespass of my body, a reflection of the settler's true identity—to take what will never be theirs and to search for pleasure and wholeness in the harm of another.

These conditions also create the parameters that dictate the way I view myself and relate to my own body. The harm of settler colonialism is so immersive, the weight of the bog is so all-encompassing, that it wounds not just our physical bodies but also our most intimate relationships inside of mind and body. As my body is held in place by thick layers of mud—pieces of people and places, and impenetrable shame—the bog seeps inside me through my permeable and delicate skin.

I spent the first three-quarters of my life trapped in the limits of my shame. As a young person, my body was violated, and I was unable to understand that the harm I experienced was inflicted upon me externally through no fault of my own. The dehumanization I felt as a young Native girl, coupled with the trespassing of my body, normalized sex as something that did not belong to me but rather to the person on the other side of it. In the captivity of shame, to feel truly good during sex was not my right, my place, or even my concern. In the context of my young disembodiment, to feel pleasure required me to travel back to a body where I was not ready to acknowledge what had happened to it. My sexuality became defined by the shame I was unable to break out of. I learned, so early on, how to perform my sexuality and my desire in order to appease others so that I did not have to be present within the experience, so that my spirit could drift away from my body and look away from how it had been harmed, so that I could feel like a human being.

The dehumanization of Indigenous peoples runs deep. The settler colonial bog holds our bodies in place through shame and violence, while seeping into our hearts to distort our capacity to give and receive love and care. When faced with such relentless dehumanization, it is only natural to search for value in other ways. Settler colonialism assigns value to people based on how much they conform to its structures of oppression. Although settlers might participate in, and contribute to, the construction of certain structures of oppression primarily for the privilege of doing so, those under the thumb of settler colonialism might also be drawn to participate for the ways in which it lends them a false sense of value and humanity. When you feel like you are not a human being, you desperately cling to the fleeting forms of value you might be able to access. As our bodies are fully submerged in the settler colonial bog, our foot is subtly steadied by a log resting on the bottom of the pond. We exhale in relief to find a tangible anchor in this muddy mess. Except the log is part and parcel of the settler colonial structure we ultimately wish to transcend.

When I was young, I found a sense of value through my appearance, and a sense of comfort through my complicity with the structure of cisheteropatriarchy. I found my humanity in the way my body and face looked, and over time, I limited my self-worth to those dimensions. In high school, I struggled with an eating disorder, yearning to fit into the Western beauty standards that determine who is worthy and valid, and also in order to benefit from the structure of fatphobia. I always cared about what I looked like and benefited from the privilege of being considered pretty in the settler colonial world, even though this privilege never shielded me completely from white supremacy—*You are so pretty, for a Native girl. My little Pocahontas. You are so exotic. You must be so proud to be beautiful and smart, considering.*

I did not have healthy sexual relationships and often sought the approval of people who did not see me as a full human being. My sexuality was defined by what the other person wanted. As a young person, I internalized myself as a non-human object. Even as an adolescent just beginning to explore my body and relationships, I internalized pleasure as the practice of letting my body satisfy another's. My very first relationship was abusive, and racially charged, with a final fight ending with the words, "I hope you burn in hell with all the other Natives."

But when I was in my early twenties, I fell deeply and madly in love with someone who actually saw me and loved me as a whole human being. It was the kind of love that didn't feel like a choice orchestrated by my shame-filled self but rather one that came from the great beyond, like some cosmic necessity. It was an incredibly painful experience to be seen for the first time and to be asked to see myself. Simple questions such as "Can I touch you? How do you like to be touched? What do you want?" made me writhe in discomfort because I could not answer them. These questions also illuminated the lack of consent that had characterized my previous relationships and experiences until this point. The muddiness of all my past traumatic experiences—the fact that I was drinking, the fact that I said no but was with a partner, the fact that I allowed an experience to happen because I was in shock—had enabled me to dismiss them so I didn't have to look at them. But now I was forced to see the truth of these experiences—the fact that I was drunk and unconscious, the memory of running half-naked into an alleyway to hide in complete distress after my partner didn't listen, the realization that I was frozen in shock because I was still a child. I couldn't look away now. This love called me back to my body, like standing on a frozen lake and hearing a distant voice calling my name across the moaning ice.

I painted my body bleeding under the full moon—the blood of these experiences, the blood of my father's experiences, the blood of my mother's experiences, the blood of my family's experiences, the blood of all my ancestors' experiences, pouring out of me and held by the pleasure I was committed to in my body.

I learned so much in my twenties, and it all started with being able to witness the truth of my experiences for the first time in my life. The work continues. Now, as I am getting older, I am again forced to confront my reliance on my body and appearance for my sense of value and humanity as I begin to be affected differently by the structure of ageism. My body is changing. My face is changing. The very beginning of these changes marks a new confrontation with the invisibilized impacts of colonialism on my sense of self. I watch my laugh lines deepen and my subconscious tells me my value and my ability to be a real human being are slipping away. I listen to my self-dialogue and hear that I will never be enough. In my conscious mind, I can feel worthy and proud of what I have accomplished and sacrificed in my life to contribute to the world around me, but in the deepest parts of me, the parts I cannot see, I still don't know how to feel completely worthy of love and pleasure and wholeness. I still don't know how to find the totality of my value and my humanity outside of my appearance and how I am perceived by others. Importantly, my experience here is an intersectional one. I am not just enmeshed in the structures of cisheteropatriarchy and ageism; I am also grappling with white supremacy as a cisgender and racialized Native woman. This isn't a conversation about reclaiming aging or beauty in a male-dominated world; this is about naming the ways that white supremacy entices us to subscribe to the structures of oppression that give colonized people a sense of humanity within a horrific context of unimaginable dehumanization. I name this so that I can transcend it.

With age also comes strength. I have now done the work to be able to bear witness. I hold parts of myself with care in my now wise hands. I stroke the hair of Quill when she was a child who at times felt so alone, the twelve-year-old Quill who was touched before puberty, the seventeen-year-old Quill who woke up not knowing what had happened the night before, the twenty-year-old Quill who was held against a wall with rage. Even the thirty-one-year-old Quill who is confronting, still, her inability to find value deep within bone and belly. I sit with them all and weep. I feel it all. Even in my brokenness, I can be whole. Vulnerability with age is a beautiful thing. Here is me—all of me.

While writing this, I moved through embarrassment and hesitation. I wondered: *Will people believe me? Will people pity me? Will I appear weak or shallow?* As someone who comes from a family that has experienced unimaginable violence, I also moved through the impulse to minimize my own experiences of harm compared to others in my family. For many years, I relied on the notion that I could handle my own experiences internally because there are so many more significant harms to remedy than those in my own body. The harms that both of my parents faced are incomprehensible in scale and horror, and I hid behind this for a long time as a way to thwart the necessity for me to deal with my own bodily experiences. But now I don't want to carry the weight of the settler colonial bog anymore—the shame, the harm, the holes in my body that are longing to be repaired. Every trespass of our bodies—no matter how big or small—matters. Every harm we experience is worthy of our tender care. I will not normalize the horror of settler colonialism by minimizing my own non-consensual experiences just because there has been so much horror around me. With age, I am able to walk out of the confines of my shame.

I think now about the intergenerational threads of resistance and profound love that run through my family. I think now about the love and labour of my mother and father, and the moment they decided to walk out of the confines of their shame. How old was my father when he decided to denounce the secrecy and silence surrounding his experience at residential school, when he decided to say, "Fuck it and fuck them, I was a child"? What work allowed my mother to tell me her experiences in a world that had never listened to her in the first place? I think about all the moments when a family member has disclosed violence to me, and the strength and love and desire to be whole that was needed in that very moment, and how that moment itself is a prayer for my wholeness. I now realize that I am not alone in this struggle or this work, however different our experiences might be. Anishinaabeg have been doing the work to love ourselves out of shame for generations. Anishinaabeg have always worked so hard to stay soft. When I truly think about the depth of love needed to carry us to this moment, I am brought to my knees.

This immensity of love and labour has allowed us to

persist and gives me the strength to fight for a life of plea-sure and wholeness. I struggle the most with the *desire* to feel pleasure. I have spent my life avoiding presence within my body because it hurts, replicating the desire of others instead of exploring my own, and convincing myself that I don't want or need true pleasure in my life. True plea-sure means stepping away from the performance of desire and pleasure that appeases an internalization of myself as a non-human object in the settler world and, instead, exploring my own intimate desires that are specific to my body, home-lands, and web of creation. Because expanding our capacity for pleasure requires our unique reclamations of presence in our bodies, it has been a gruelling and painful process of growing closer with my body that carries stories of harm that I have not wanted to sit with until now. As someone who struggles with desire—the desire to experience true pleasure from both myself and others, the ability to feel worthy and deserving of true pleasure—I have come to rely on specific tools to help me get closer to a life of wholeness.

One of these tools is to remember pleasure is an indi-vidual practice that has collective implications within the context of settler colonialism. Our pleasure is never just our own when our bodies contain so much of all that we are and all that we will be. Anishinaabe pleasure is felt individually but ripples outward to the collective. When our bodies feel good, our ancestors laugh in delight and our homelands tremble in gratitude. When our bodies feel good, we are harder to remove from our land. I find great strength in reminding myself that the designation of who gets to receive pleasure and feel deserving of pleasure is always political.

While I might find it hard to wake up every day and choose pleasure for myself, I find it effortless to wake up every day and choose pleasure and wholeness for my people. I use this subtle shift in thinking to remedy the negative feedback loop of trying to love myself within the dehumanization of settler colonialism that has limited my ability to do so in the first place. In other words, I might struggle with the motivation to fight for pleasure in my own body, but when I remember that pleasure is collective, I find the motivation to love myself as one of my responsibilities to restore Anishinaabe rights to whole bodies, lives, and spirits.

Another tool is the understanding that pleasure is political, and that this, in turn, means reclaiming what pleasure means to us as Anishinaabe people. Settler colonialism promotes a relationship to pleasure that is limited by the physical realm and governed by the logic of cisheteropatriarchy. In the colonial world, pleasure is about the physical body experiencing good sensations, with the prioritization of pleasure in cisgender, heterosexual, male bodies. Stigma is one of the factors that sustains this power dynamic, shaming expressions of sexuality and pleasure in those who do not benefit from cisheteropatriarchy. As an Indigenous person, I feel this stigma tenfold because of how instrumental the hypersexualization of Indigenous bodies has been to the settler colonial project. We are constantly sexualized externally, but when we express our sexuality on our own terms, we are shallow, disgusting, and even threatening. Many people in our communities have internalized the colonial relationship to pleasure, writing off Indigenous people's expressions of sex and pleasure as hedonistic, inappropriate, and vulgar.

But pleasure from an Anishinaabe perspective is so much more than the physical. Our bodies are so much more than our physical containers. Pleasure in our bodies is healing the bodies of our ancestors, convening with our web of relationality, and reclaiming the wholeness that is integral to who we are as Anishinaabe people. Remembering this collectivist approach to pleasure gives me the strength to confront the stigma I face as an Indigenous woman exploring her desire, pleasure, and wholeness within the settler colonial world that hates and harms us.

I first encountered the power of being unpalatable to settler colonialism when I painted my body feeling pleasure. I painted *kwe becomes the moon, touches herself so she can feel full again*, which depicts me pleasuring myself while menstruating. After I posted the painting on social media, I was immediately barraged with unsolicited messages from white women telling me I was disgusting and white men mobilizing white supremacist Facebook groups to disclose who I was and where I lived. This imagery of a Native woman feeling pleasure was so unpalatable to the colonial gaze that it invoked visceral reactions. Even just the idea of our bodies feeling pleasure is threatening enough to rupture the settler colonial fabric that is always more fragile than it seems.

I use the tool of unpalatability as a cue in my daily life to reorient my sense of value around my identity as an Anishinaabe person who transcends settler colonialism. If someone expresses disgust for me, which happens not only when I express my sexuality but also when I am just existing, I can feel power in that rather than shame. As someone who has struggled with orienting myself toward subconsciously appeasing the settler gaze to lessen my felt dehumanization, this allows me to reclaim my own system of value that celebrates my ability to upset settler colonialism through my body and my existence. I stand before settler colonialism in all my unpalatable glory; it cannot even bear to look at me, and I am free at last.

My final tool to tend to a life of pleasure and wholeness is remembering that pleasure is also a practice. Rather than pleasure being a stagnant goal with an end and a beginning, pleasure is a fluid portal to wholeness that ebbs and flows like the waters of my body. The prerequisite to pleasure is desire, and to feel desire, you must value your body and yourself as worthy of wholeness. In the times when I cannot access the desire to be whole and full, or worthy of love and care in my body, I turn to pleasure as a practice to get me there. Quite literally, I practise. In the times when I cannot desire my own fullness, I turn to my body as a teacher. I throw myself at the feet of my own body and ask her to make me whole, and she always does.

Pleasure is both the state of being I must desire and the methodology by which I can get there. With each droplet of water from my body, with each vibration that echoes like the hum of the universe inside me, with each inevitable rejection of my own dehumanization, my body always knows how to make me whole, even if just for a moment. Acknowledging pleasure as a practice means remembering this is a strategy in itself to grow closer to the ability to desire pleasure in its fullest sense—to wake up every day and choose to feel whole and good in our bodies. To wake up every day and feel whole and good in our bodies for our parents who could not. To wake up every day and feel whole and good in our bodies for our ancestors who are praying for us to do this work. To wake up every day and feel whole and good in our bodies for our children who long to see their parents feeling joy and delighting in their sweet existence.

Pleasure from an Anishinaabe perspective is the bridging of the physical with everything beyond ourselves. Our skin is bound to the stars that we come from, sewn together with tender stitches of ink made of earth. Our hearts are like the rocks that sing to us, pulsing with the drumbeat of time immemorial. Our blood contains the water of our homelands, carried by the currents of celestial breath from the great beyond. Making our bodies feel good is not just about the physical sensations we feel in our bodies; it is about those physical sensations radiating outward to touch all the elements that have prayed for our wholeness.

When we touch ourselves, the stars quiver in ecstasy. When we feel pleasure in our bodies, the rocks start to sing. When we become whole, the water flows and our ancestors gather to celebrate our ability to feel good and worthy and loved despite the violence, the harm, and the settler colonial bog.

Under the full moon, I weep. I throw myself at the feet of my own body because tonight I am tired. My tears fall down my cheeks and warm my face, some of them trailing underneath my jaw and down my neck. They start to feel good. Deep inside body, the fluttering of a fish calling me back to sensation. Deep inside heart, my ancestors throw wood onto my embers, and they spark and crackle into fire. My breath starts to quicken, and with each exhalation, my breath is joined by the smoke inside me. I deserve to feel good. The smoke surrounds my body in a thick fog as the moon sings to me. The fish jumps to break the surface of my body, and its ripples reach the great beyond.

And then, she came to me. Giizik was born. On the early morning of a warm August day, I felt the waters of my homelands rush out of me with the force of creation's breath. These waters inside me were composed of the joyous tears of my ancestors, ancient sturgeon swimming through the starscapes where my daughter had just sat with all our spirits—primordial creation traversing time and space to hold this tiny being in holy reverence. When these waters spilled from my body, they brought with them the knowledge of the great beyond and the tangible feeling of wholeness. As soon as my daughter was born, I understood what I was inheriting through her existence—the tools to be whole. As soon as my daughter was born, I understood my responsibility to shape her inheritance from my own body. As soon as she exited my body, I felt the lingering songs of the ancient great beyond rippling across my flesh and inviting me to dance in all that I am and all that I can be.

Bringing Indigenous life into this world is a tender embrace between ecstasy and grief. I look at my daughter's toddler body that is so free and whole, and I cannot help but anticipate its harm because of our immersion in the settler colonial bog. I look at my daughter's smile that is so otherworldly in its joy, and I cannot help but notice how my own laughter longs to be as deep. I look at our family tree extending far into the galaxies that shine down upon us, and I can intergenerationally trace both unbounded love and unimaginable harms specific to our bodies and pleasure. I long for these harms to end with my daughter, but I cannot be certain they will. The ability to be whole through my own fullness and sense of expansive pleasure is no longer a lofty goal but a necessity to ensure the protection of my daughter's sacred wholeness.

The grief of anticipated harm on our children's tiny bodies is so heavy. My heart breaks a thousand times by the time she is three. Settler colonialism is relentless and cunning, and I have learned that whole and full Anishinaabe bodies feeling worthy of pleasure and goodness are deeply terrifying to the settler state. And so, I brace for the harms that will affect my daughter's body, her wholeness, and her ability to feel the expansive pleasure that connects us to the great beyond.

In order to protect Giizik's bodily sovereignty, I started to teach her about consent from the youngest of ages. We would practise holding boundaries and cueing for consent and non-consent while encountering just how often adults wildly ignore the boundaries of children. Teaching Giizik about consent also forced me to confront the ways I still, as an adult, am uncomfortable with holding boundaries. I noticed my hesitation to step in to help Giizik assert a body boundary when it was awkward or tense. I took lots of deep breaths and drew upon the strength to do this for her, even if I still could not do it for myself. We practised body literacy, learning the names of all the body parts while rejecting the shame that surrounds bodies, pleasure, and intimacy. This constituted the foundation of what I knew would be a life-long complexity of protecting and nurturing my daughter's wholeness in her body. But my role as her parent cannot be compartmentalized to simply helping her protect her body; it is also my responsibility to change the material conditions of the world around us such that wholeness is a right she can freely live out.

I began to realize that I am such a big part of her world. I began to realize that the real work would be reclaiming my own wholeness and giving my daughter the living embodiment of a mother who is able to delight in the sweetness of creation contained within her beautiful body. I began to realize the significance of this work—what it would mean to break our inherited disembodiment that has travelled throughout generations truncating us from our wholeness; what it would mean to insist on a life of pleasure just one generation from the residential school system; what it would mean to have a child grow up with an example of flourishing wholeness. Our sense of pleasure and fullness in our bodies is never an individual or selfish reclamation; it is a collective act that stirs the sacred smoke binding Anishinaabe bodies to all that we are.

I think of all the moments when I feel like I am going to burst with love and admiration for Giizik. I think of all the moments when I look at her and feel so honoured to walk this life with her. I think of all the moments when I simply delight in her existence, bubbling up with a love so ferocious. And I ask myself: "Why don't you feel this way about yourself? Your time in this specific body is fleeting and you must delight in this existence." And so, I begin a practice where I find those same moments with myself. I look down at my body and feel so honoured to be alive for one more day. I look down at my body and feel like I am going to burst with love and admiration and gratitude and humility at what a sweet and tender embrace my body lends me in this complex life. I look down at my body and weep.

And so, I work so hard to be whole—for her and for me and for all Anishinaabeg. Despite the distance between my body and self, I return in the cold night to hold my body. I take my body in my arms and caress my dark hair, and when I run my fingers through it, the murmurs of ancestors escape into the night around us. I trace the curvature of my body—smooth and soft parts meeting the uneven and unpredictable parts of thigh—warmth returning with each touch. I travel the long road between body and self for Giizik, and one day for me, repairing the ruptures and erosions of my body from the settler colonial bog.

My body, you are so soft and flexible, so strong and sturdy; every day I remain with you is a prayer answered. My body, you are the keeper of my wholeness, spilling out the waters of my homelands and the great beyond to teach me about my own fullness. I will work so hard to be whole so that, just maybe, the harms can end with Giizik, and if they don't, so that I can be whole enough to hold her through it all, that I can be so whole that when she is not, I have enough wholeness for both of us.

Chapter 8

On Wholeness and Responsibility
*Palestine called me back to my body
and I danced with all that I am, for us*

*On a night in October 2023, I had a dream that did not come
from me. I was hiding from an unknown army and there were
people around me trembling in fear—babies, children, men,
and women. And then, I heard it. The low rumbling above
us of what I knew was a bomb. I looked up at the ceiling, and
in the most visceral sense, I felt my body fill with a dread
unknown to me in this life. I thought to myself that I am not
scared to die, but I am scared to die under this rubble, in
this way. I thought about the large pieces of heavy concrete
that would bury my body. When I woke up, I wept. I knew I
had travelled somewhere that night. The body is always the
technology of our sacred empathy.*

 Palestine taught me that wholeness is not just our right;
our journey toward wholeness supports our responsibility
for collective liberation. Palestine called me back into my
body in ways that I had never experienced before. Palestine
activated a sense of otherworldly responsibility and worldbuilding informed by the stardust that I come from, and my

ancestors whispered in my ear that I must be embodied in order to meet these responsibilities.

What followed October 7, 2023, marked an escalation in the seventy-six-year-old genocidal occupation of Palestine. I was just starting to write this book when everything I knew flew into pieces. In the ensuing months, the whole world bore witness to the unmasked brutality of settler colonialism. On the small screens of our phones, we witnessed every scream, every face, every massacre, and every minute detail of the horrors of this genocide. The scale and scope of violence was incomprehensible, and our capacity to witness was made infinite by the bravery and resilience of Palestinians on the ground.

On a night in November, I had a dream that did not come from me. I dreamed that I was a man hiding with my family, doing everything I could to keep them safe. Desperation. We were hiding in a small closet when they found us. One of the soldiers held a gun to my forehead, and the world slowed down enough for me to process it all. He shot me point-blank in front of my family. I woke up and wept.

The universe is so vast that our earth is often overlooked by the spiritual entities that we know roam the sky. Our galactic spirits dance among the stars, attending to their business, looking down upon us only every now and then. But the violence of this moment was so shattering that it reached into the great beyond and we were noticed. When Israel bombed Al-Ahli Hospital, the spirits at the farthest corners of the galaxy stirred in pain and tilted their ethereal heads toward our small world, a low wail traversing the great beyond. On that night, the totality of the universe retched and wailed at a violence so unnatural that it echoed beyond time and space.

I will never forget the image of the press conference outside the hospital—doctors surrounded by shrouded bodies, eyes wide with desperation, holding delicately the small and limp body of an infant. Deep in my bones that still have ancient stardust in them, I could feel the low wail of the universe meeting me in sacred rage, the smoke swirling inside my body with the presence of spirits being awoken from the farthest of stars. The great beyond trembles in rage for Palestine.

Palestine, my bones ache for you, and my ancestors join me in my rage and grief.

Palestine, I could never look away; you have me in my entirety.

On a night in December, I awoke to the sound of my bedroom door rattling. I sat up, perplexed, and slowly registered that no windows were open and there was no reasonable explanation. Sometimes, the spirits let us know they are there. I listened to my door rattle aggressively for thirty minutes, the sound of the universe trembling in rage and grief beside me, and I felt relief. The movement of my door signalled a presence from my ancestors and spirits—We are here with you, in your grief, in your responsibilities. We too are bearing witness.

Everything flew into pieces during this time. Everything in my life stopped and changed. I could not write. I could not paint. My creative practice felt wholly irrelevant in the face of an unfolding extermination of an Indigenous people. Like being awoken from a slumber, I suddenly felt as though my entire life was fraudulent as I was forced to confront the normalization of my own complicity in capitalism and colonialism, even as an Indigenous person doing anti-colonial work for my own community. I was overwhelmed by the juxtaposition of witnessing genocide in real time alongside fulfilling my daily responsibilities that held no meaning beyond my survival in the settler colonial world. With razor-sharp clarity, I realized that, despite being an Anishinaabe person resisting the settler colonial world, I spent so much of my daily life floating around in, and tolerating, the settler colonial bog.

Suddenly, I wanted no part in it. I was repulsed by the parts of my life I had previously accepted. I began to understand that my tolerance of settler colonialism here on Turtle Island was more extensive than I had realized, and that this tolerance is what allows the machinery of empire to continue.

Palestine swept me away, submerging my body completely within a new scale of resistance.

For Anishinaabeg, our dreams bind us to our sacred responsibilities. Our dreams are the doorways to the great beyond, our ancestors, and the universe unfolding within them. These dreams did not come from my own mind. They were offerings from my spirit helpers to ground me in an unshakeable empathy and a deep understanding of the scope and urgency of my responsibilities to Palestine in my felt body. Our bodies have always deeply terrified settler colonialism.

My body became my greatest teacher. Like in the old creation story my great-grandma told where the woman's body filled with the swells of creation, my body had to transform to hold my welling grief. My heart was the first part of me to grow. I watched the steadfast men of Palestine comfort children who were stuck under the rubble, refusing to let them die alone. I watched them collapse into each other's arms with exhaustion and relief when they were able to rescue people from the ruins, and my heart began to bulge. I watched Elders weep at the foot of their destroyed homes turned into rubble, and my heart risked bursting. I was the old woman of creation sitting by a river filling her body with the grief of the universe, but my own ancestors were working at the edge of my body. They hummed and sang the same songs they used to comfort their own fearful children during our massacres, while they stretched and massaged my swelling tissues in order for my heart to grow to make space for the grief I had to carry. Every part of my body expanded and contorted against my impending breach. And in this new-found breadth of my physicality—heart swelling with the tears of my ancestors, mind at the brink of rupture with the incomprehensibility of the violence we were witnessing—my body held it all and called me home to answer to my responsibilities.

I marvelled at my body's ability to expand and transform to meet the current moment. The grief that filled my body was so visceral that I could not hide it deep within my flesh like I do with my own grief and my people's grief. The grief that filled my body was so alive with urgency that I could not turn away from it even though it hurt. The grief that filled my body was so collective that when I screamed, my voice was met with the wailing of my ancestors, the ancient moaning of our spirit kin, and the sound of water rushing over rapids as they all made their hurried way to our world.

Sometimes, this grief would spill out of my engorged heart or full eyes and I would rupture the fraudulent normalcy of the settler colonial world. Sometimes, I would scan the eyes of people in the grocery store hoping to meet another tear-filled gaze so I could feel less alone. Most importantly, the grief that filled my body demanded action. As the grief filled my shifting body, I was moved into sustained worldbuilding.

As we organized, I traced the different approaches in our communities. We had so much to learn from one another. Settler colonialism has never wanted us to truly see one another. Palestinian organizers—unified, disciplined, urgent, and fact-based in order to dispel the Zionist propaganda machine. Anishinaabe organizers—relational, existing in multiplicities, taking the time, deeply spiritual. All have a place. Our role was quickly illuminated: Let us hold our Palestinian kin through this moment. Let us share what has allowed us to persist through genocide for generations, on this land. Let us make space for your grief. Let us make space for the relationships that will sustain the front-line work. Let our spirits hold you. Let our homelands hold you. Let our ceremonies care for you. Let us hold the pieces of you that are breaking, so that we all can continue. Take a moment. It is okay to cry. Look, I am crying with you. We will hold you. Look, the spirits are with us now. Look, the smoke in the

lodge has been lit. Our homelands love you so. Let your tears
fall on our land so that it knows exactly how to care for you.

Somewhere in the thick of the fall of 2023, when I spent
my days glued to my phone, driving with my three-year-
old daughter to various organizing meetings, and weeping
uncontrollably when there was a moment to breathe, I felt it.
I realized that even within the crushing pain of this moment,
I was fully embodied. For the first time since I was a child,
I felt fully present in my body for an extended period of
time. Palestine was calling for me to be whole. My ancestors,
trembling with the rage of the great beyond, were calling me
back into my body with a ferocity I had only experienced
in fleeting moments. Palestine dispelled my intergenerational and deeply rooted disembodiment. Palestine woke
up Indigenous peoples across the globe and showed us how
we must resist.

Perhaps I could never be this whole for myself or my own
community, drowning in the layers of shame and nuanced
complexities surrounding our settler colonial experience,
which has been sustained over many more generations
than in younger settler colonies. But I can be this whole for
Palestine. I can be this whole for my global kin who endure
the same clutches of imperialism and settler colonialism.
The spirits of the universe visit us from the farthest corners
of the galaxy to tell us that it is happening again, all over
the globe. My ancestors scream, *It cannot happen again.*
Perhaps this is the solution for the inertia that prevents us
from collectively reaching genuine and sustained practices
of joint struggle—the innate ability to do for others what we

cannot do for ourselves, the clarity of our resistance when it is shown to us outside the layers of the settler colonial bog that have submerged us here on Turtle Island for so very long, convening with our effortless and expansive empathy that always orients us toward worldbuilding. In this way we can learn once again to feel that empathy for ourselves, and to become whole for us too.

I think of how starkly this revelation stands in opposition to the inertia of whiteness, which prevents those complicit in the structure of whiteness to move into sustained action for the building of a more just world. This inertia eclipses any sense of responsibility that extends beyond one's own individual experience and impact. The way to move past white inertia is to cultivate a sense of sacred empathy, the kind that I hope resides in the hearts of all human beings. To move past white inertia is to return to the swirling smoke inside you, to feel extended networks of relationality that you must work to belong to and be accountable to. The work of Indigenous people to move beyond our inertia to take up sustained practices of joint struggle is to let other kin care for the parts of us that we cannot. We can sustain liberatory and collective joint struggle by finally seeing each other amid the imperial storm and finding wholeness in and through one another.

The totality of creation, the voices of my ancestors, the soft breath of my three-year-old, and the people of Palestine called me back into my body. They asked me to be whole, and quite simply, I needed to be whole in order to meet this moment and to be able to carry it. I needed to be embodied so that my body could transform and so that parts of me would eventually rupture to birth new worlds. I realized that to be whole is not an idyllic state of euphoria and joy, or the end goal of liberation, but rather, it is simply the ability to be present in our bodies enough to be in dialogue with our expansive relationality. Our wholeness can be characterized by grief and pain, so long as we are convening with all the relations that hold us so tenderly. The fires inside my body were lit, and the sacred smoke was so thick that it permeated every orifice of my being. Our wholeness is necessary for us to attain any semblance of our liberation.

How much more can they take? How much more can we take? How much more can I take? I take a breath and place what I just witnessed in my bones, beside my ancestors' stories, beside all the other scenes I will never forget. And my bones simply grow and become more sturdy. I remember that I am not just me—I am everything and beyond. My body is teaching me how to hold and be whole—a political act of resistance and liberation.

The infrastructure of settler colonialism is always governed by its rampant compartmentalizations. These compartmentalizations attempt to remove the physical body from all that it is connected to in order to instill the individualism that is at the heart of settler colonialism. We are taught to compartmentalize ourselves from our larger communities, from our homelands, and from our ancestors while orienting our responsibilities toward the individual or the nuclear family. In this context of hyper-individualism, our internalized compartmentalizations run deep. Even our activism can be compartmentalized from an expansive global practice of joint struggle to our localized context, governed by a hierarchy that places our community's struggle before another's. In this case, solidarity is something we do when we can, but it is not a necessity. Our activism is further compartmentalized in the West when we disconnect external and internal forms of resistance from each other, operating from a hierarchy that values the work we do outside of ourselves at the expense of the vital internal work necessary for liberation. Palestine spilled over all these compartmentalizations, demanding a reclamation of our holistic resistance.

As I became activated—spiritually and materially—by the escalation of the genocide in Gaza, my daily life began to feel increasingly absurd. I would acutely notice the parts of my day that I spent fulfilling obligatory mundane responsibilities that were not tied to my greater purpose or the justice of creation. I would walk in the park holding back tears, imagining that everyone around me was doing the same because I could not bear to live in a world where they were not. I wanted to scream and wail in every public place I moved through, the uncanny normalcy of everyone around me like a dull suffocation. The new-found absurdity in my life signalled a shift in my internal landscape in which my tolerance for my own participation in settler colonialism was waning. Even the previously sweet parts of life became tainted with the undeniable grief welling in my body. I watched my daughter's first dance recital and I was overcome with emotion as toddlers stumbled around the stage in their sacred innocence that was currently being stolen from so many children in Palestine. The only actions that made sense were giving my daughter a loving home and organizing for a free Palestine.

The unmasking of the absurdity and mockery of our lives in the imperial core is a gift that we cannot let go to waste. Like lifting an impenetrable veil, Palestine taught us that we must demand so much more.

My discontent with the veneer of normalcy of my life in the imperial core is a rejection of the compartmentalization of my activism that would consider Palestine a separate issue from my own community and one that I should contribute to externally. It has been written, deep in my Anishinaabe bones, to fight for the children of Palestine as if they were my own. It has been written, through my dreams and the spirits who visit me, to carry an embodied responsibility to our Palestinian kin. And as I have been swept away by my own sense of wholeness, so many parts of my life have become absurd.

I don't want to live in a world that is governed by settler colonialism while my community struggles and dies. I don't want to live in a world where I don't know my neighbours and everyone is separated and lonely. I don't want to live in a world where my time is stolen from me by immersive capitalism. I don't want to live in a world where my daughter is at daycare for seven hours of every day. But for the most part, I have tolerated these conditions because they are so layered, insidious, and seemingly inescapable.

But now, the violence that is always at the heart of settler colonialism has been made undeniable and visceral, and I can trace it and watch it. I don't want to live in a world where I am forced to act normal while I watch children die on my phone, and so, I sharpen my intolerance and my life becomes absurd. I don't want to live in a world where I watch the same horrors that my ancestors endured at the bloody hands of colonialism, and so I don't tolerate it and my daily life becomes even more absurd. The awareness of all these absurdities signals the beginning of unease, unrest, repulsion, and intolerance for the normalcy of our daily lives in the settler colony. Considering this is one of the largest roadblocks to our liberation in the imperial core—the lull of comfort and normalcy that generates the tolerance for our own oppression—the magnitude of this feat is worth naming. Palestine deeply radicalized us and showed us the absurdity of our lives in the settler colony, and how to move from tolerance to intolerance, for them and for us.

I feel that my life in the settler colonial world is absurd because I am whole, and I can feel the visceral dialogue with my ancestors and spirits fed to me from the great beyond rooting me in my true purpose that does not consent to the hollowness and violence of the colonial world. I feel that my life in the settler colonial world is a mockery because I deeply understand that my tolerance and complicity in the settler colony of Canada has everything to do with the genocide in Palestine. I feel that my life is absurd in all the intimacies of my daily life because I deeply understand that true liberation is both an external and an internal practice, and experiencing my personal daily life as intolerable creates the conditions for sustained and revolutionary sacrifice in the material realm. It is going to take so much sacrifice to build the liberated worlds that we need. We must find the strength to make our lives as we know them completely unrecognizable as we shift into new collective ways of being. The mockery of our lives in the West is a gift that we cannot let go to waste.

We are all indebted to what Palestine has taught us—a gift of immense clarity in the settler colonial bog that submerges our bodies here in the West, the shock of cold water splashed across our faces to call us back into our bodies, the slumber of mass disembodiment disrupted to remind us of what is possible and what needs to be possible for collective liberation. We don't have to live in a world continuously built on genocide and unimaginable harm. We don't have to live in a world where we fear for the safety of children, and pray they can at least pass away alongside a relative. We don't have to live in a world where we must fight to protect the sanctity of our men's bodies and dignity. We don't have to live in a world where even our babies are not safe from the horror. We don't have to live in an increasingly absurd world governed by hollow capitalism and the theft of our time and connectivity. We don't have to accept the manufactured inertia that hampers our collective ability to move into sustained joint struggle.

The building of a new world, where we are all free and whole, is worth the immense sacrifices it will take to get there. The building of a new world is our only way forward. We have everything we need inside our bodies to build this new world. My grandchildren and great-grandchildren will know the stories of Palestine and how they woke us up.

The totality of the universe trembles in rage. I feel it, in my bones and body and in my dreams and with my spirit helpers.

The universe rages because it has so much love. My ancestors rage from the great beyond because they have so much love. I rage because I have such a burning love. Neither the cosmic nor the earthly impact of a single martyr will be erased. The power of each martyr I have witnessed will ripple throughout generations of Anishinaabeg, through our bodies and the stardust that we come from. Each martyr we have witnessed will reach Indigenous peoples across the globe, waking us up from our forced slumber. I wish to say it out loud: We will always honour you.

The genocide in Gaza is unprecedented in the ways that we are all able to bear witness to every single moment of it. Through social media and the unfaltering determination of both the journalists and the people of Gaza who upload their first-hand footage, we witness every atrocity as it happens, in real time. Many of these scenes will live within me forever. I mention some of them here not to foreground Palestinian trauma, but rather to insist on the continued visibility of these realities and to name the impact that these people have on me that will ripple into the farthest corners of the universe. Reem in her grandfather's arms while he touches her hair to his chin lives in my heart. The infant Mahmoud taking his last breaths while dying of starvation split me into pieces. The premature babies who were left to slowly die alone in their incubators is something my brain will never fully comprehend. A man and his baby shot down in the street, the man reaching to caress his dead child before he passes, is otherworldly in its sorrow. These people and these moments must live within us forever. As witnesses, we carry these stories now, and we must insist that they move us to action in order to usher in the world that we need.

The role of being a witness to the genocide in Gaza was a topic of contention in the West during the early months of the escalation. In a very broad sense, there were three groups of people—those who refused to engage or witness, those who were steadfast in their responsibility to witness, and those who fell somewhere in between. Despite Palestinians on the ground quite literally begging people to bear witness to the atrocities, many in the West turned away. There was a dominant narrative, largely forwarded by white people, that they don't want or need to watch the horrific footage coming out of Gaza. Importantly, this was connected to their ability and indeed privilege to disengage from a sense of responsibility. While some turned away on the basis of their racism and inability to see Palestinians as human beings, others, whom we might call moderate liberals, argued that bearing witness threatened their well-being or capacity to live their lives in normalcy. I want to speak back to this moderate liberal grouping from an Anishinaabe understanding of the act of witnessing as a foundation to our systems of worldbuilding.

From an Anishinaabe understanding, witnessing is not simply a neutral act of observing our surroundings. Witnessing is inherently political and spiritual—the foundation of our processes of building worlds full of justice and liberation. Witnessing, in an Indigenous framework, is not a passive practice but a responsibility—a critical engagement with the world around us so that we can transform it to better hold all of creation.

Witnessing happens on multiple levels. We witness the natural world and take note of our animal, plant, and spirit kin. We witness our parents and family to better understand the legacies we must continue and the ones we must transcend. We witness our broader communities, in their strengths and in their sufferings, to determine what is needed. When we have important ceremonies or life events, we call on witnesses who carry this moment in time to ripple throughout our communities. Lastly, we witness our ancestors, both through our living memory and through our ceremonies, as we weave their knowledge into our world.

When something earth-shattering happens, something as monumental as a live-streamed genocide, it is our responsibility to bear witness. How we choose to bear witness is entirely up to each individual, but from an Anishinaabe perspective, it is essential for us to bear witness in a way that positions us within an activation of our sense of world-building. Our responsibility to bear witness does not mean that every single one of us has to watch every video, but it does mean that we all have to ensure we are witnessing enough to activate our deeper sense of responsibility that leads us to sustained action.

When the footage of the genocide in Gaza started to proliferate on mainstream social media, I remember my instinctive aversion to it. I would see something horrific, close my eyes, take a deep breath, and tell myself that I do not need to witness Palestinian suffering to activate my care and action. But over the following days, I felt called to be a witness. I thought of the people uploading this footage of their loved ones, begging the world to at least be a witness, and I felt my body expanding to meet the current moment. I knew I could hold it all, and I also knew that these stories needed to live in my bones.

I envisioned my own ancestors' suffering and horror. And I envisioned my own ancestors' suffering and horror as though in a time when it could be live-streamed. What if Anishinaabe parents were uploading footage of their children who were taken to residential school being raped and thrown into mass graves for all the world to see? What would it feel like, and what would it mean, for people to choose not to watch those videos, for people to turn away? I am so sturdy when my ancestors gather in my bones. Come place the stories in me, and they will birth a beautiful future.

Bearing witness to the genocide in Gaza was both deeply spiritual and radicalizing for me. It was also entirely disruptive, fragmenting my life into many pieces that I still have not put back together. I suspect that many chose not to bear witness because of this disruptiveness. You cannot be the same after witnessing the intricacies of genocide in real time. But that is exactly the point. I would lie beside my sleeping three-year-old daughter paralyzed with the weight of my love for her and the simultaneous extinguishment of so many little worlds full of love in Palestine. I would play with my daughter real silly and suddenly overflow with tears to see the joy and innocence in her eyes. I experienced a painful distance between people I considered friends and comrades, as our ability to connect disintegrated as they chose to look away or stay silent. And as a single mother, I ended up in a precarious financial position, my material life disrupted as much as my internal world.

Bearing witness was so full of urgency that I began to dedicate entire days to working for a free Palestine simply because I could not bear to sit with inaction. Bearing witness disrupts our lives so much that we become moved to action, despite the sacrifice that it requires of us. Bearing witness is always a foundational component of worldbuilding, and what we bear witness to in Gaza demands a complete overhaul of our current world. To be a witness for Gaza and to be Anishinaabe is to let our bodies become sacred archives that will create the blueprint for a more just future.

There is an ontological difference between an Indigenous and Western approach to the act of witnessing. This difference stems from the settler colonial compartmentalization of life, particularly the body, from all the elements of creation that it comes from. The Western gaze understands the horrific footage in Gaza as something separate, distinct, and removed from the individual watching that footage. This gaze externalizes itself from the images, thus allowing the individual to conceive of this horror as something completely separate from themselves. The individual in the West might choose to ignore the footage on the basis that it doesn't concern them or, at best, feel sad *for* the people in the video. The ontological separation of the self from creation allows for the externalization of struggle that permits non-engagement in all its various forms. Even an individual in the West who cares and wants to help might find themselves paralyzed by the manufactured hopelessness of the settler colonial world that has removed people from their capacity to worldbuild. The structures of power and privilege of settler colonialism work hard to restrict the individual so that they cannot even conceive of their inherent ability to change the world around them.

In contrast, the Indigenous gaze does not consider the individual to be separate from the expansive web of creation that surrounds them. In bearing witness to the footage of Gaza, I feel no separation or space between myself and what I am witnessing because we are bound together by our world and the expansive relationality of our existence. The suffering I bear witness to is deeply interconnected to my own body, my ancestors, my homelands, and our shared starscape and world.

As an Anishinaabe person, I do not feel sad *for* the people in the videos, and nor do I want to help them as an externalized group of people separate from myself. As an Anishinaabe person, I feel a responsibility, fed from my deepest sense of purpose, my ancestors, and the spirit helpers who join me in this critical moment, to create a world for my kin that will not produce the harmful realities I am witnessing. Rather than feeling sad for people, I feel grief because my body experiences their loss as a loss to our collective world. Rather than feeling hopeless, I feel activated. I understand that every action or inaction I take shapes our world, and I feel empowered to create a world outside this mess. To take action is not a choice. I cannot choose when or how to engage because the responsibility lives in me, encapsulated within every minute of every day.

Settler colonialism relies on the hyper-individualism at the heart of our society to remove people from their responsibilities, even when witnessing something as overtly horrifying as a genocide. Settler colonialism also relies on the manufactured hopelessness of its citizens that stems from the compartmentalization of people from their larger webs of creation. This manufactured hopelessness ontologically confines people to a place of inaction—they cannot even comprehend that every minutia of their daily life contributes to the building of our world.

A foundational part of dismantling settler colonialism and, in particular, white supremacy, is for those who benefit from it the most to challenge its worldview. Yet another gift Palestine has given us is the clarity to see the ways we have been robbed of our purpose and responsibility that extend far beyond the boundaries of the individual. We must move beyond feeling sad *for* the people experiencing the horrors of the empire we benefit from to feeling grief for the kin of our shared world that we have created and that our children will inherit—so much so that our bodies transform before our very eyes, insisting on our wholeness. Learning from this moment means bearing witness so that we may be moved to action, rejecting the individualism of settler colonialism and reclaiming our responsibility to build a better world for everyone.

To those who care deeply but cannot move into genuine action, do you realize what they have taken from you? Having true purpose in this life that extends beyond the frail walls of capitalism keeps me warm on the coldest of nights. Living out my responsibilities fed lovingly to me by my ancestors is the greatest honour, even if it costs me. I cannot fathom anything

more beautiful than sacrificing for the world around us, love
spilling over every orifice of my body. Do you realize what
they have taken from you, and how you can reach out and
take it back?

To witness the genocide in Palestine holds different dimensions for an Anishinaabe person who persists
through genocide here on Turtle Island. The stories of my
ancestors and even my family live within me in relatively
abstract ways. The vibrant colours of our suffering only truly
exist through my own lived experience and what I have
witnessed first-hand, the rest being story and the dull ache
of my ancestors' pain in my bones. What I have witnessed
of the genocide in Palestine colours all these stories out of
my imagination and into real life. The children I watched
starve to death speak to me of what my ancestors looked
like in their final moments, what their parents looked like
in complete and utter desperation and helplessness. The
Elders I have watched cry beside their demolished homes
speak to me of what expressions might have been on my
ancestors' faces as they were displaced from their homelands. The brave men of Palestine moving with such strength
speak to me of the Anishinaabe men who whispered, "It is
a good day to die," before offering their bodies to our resistance. And the tenacity and will to live contained within
the joyous smile of a Palestinian child, the teacher holding
class amid the rubble, the young men doing backflips across
their homelands, speak to me of the unfaltering strength
and love of my own ancestors who fought so hard for us to
live in joy and fullness.

The similarities between our experiences is, at times, quite literal. Like a spherical scaffolding encasing the earth, empire connects our communities viscerally and across time and space. Settler colonial nations such as Canada, the United States, Israel, and the United Kingdom are the strongholds of empire. They rely on each other to bolster their respective power and support the overarching domination of imperialism. They not only share tactics of dispossession and violence; they are the same machinery. Although the specifics of our experiences of settler colonialism are different, the heart of the struggle is the same. The burning of olive trees is akin to the killing of buffalo on the plains. The demonization of Palestinian men as violent terrorists is akin to the way our men have been labelled terrorists for fighting for our land. The unimaginable torture of Palestinian political prisoners is akin to the grotesque experimentation on and torture of our children in residential schools. We are bound together through the same machinery of empire that uses the same techniques of violence.

There is no greater way to illustrate the interconnections between Indigenous people on Turtle Island and the Palestinian struggle than to speak with reverence of Hind Rajab. Hind was a six-year-old girl who was fleeing Gaza City with her family in a car when Israeli tanks opened fire and killed everyone except for Hind. While she was trapped in the car with her dead family members, the world listened to her fearful calls to the Red Crescent asking for them to come rescue her. For days, I thought of her. For days, the world waited to hear if she would be rescued. Thinking of Hind brought me to my knees. I felt absolutely overcome, like my body was rupturing with a tidal wave of blood and rage and grief. When I thought of Hind, so much spilled out of me. A small child fighting for her life in a sea of death and destruction, the unspeakable trauma of being surrounded by dead family, the horror of being the only one who survived, a child alone.

Then I remembered the story my dad has always told me about one of our ancestors—my great-great-grandma. When she was eight years old her entire family was massacred. She hid under their dead bodies for days to survive, and then walked alone from the United States until she eventually came all the way up to Northwestern Ontario. Her story was so similar to Hind's. I thought of everything that came from just one of my ancestors—all the ferocity of love and strength that has enabled me to be here today so that when I heard the story of little Hind, I would be brought to my knees. So that when I think about Hind, my body ruptures with the low moaning of the great beyond such that I can channel my deepest responsibilities. I thought of what kind of descendant of my ancestor I would be if Hind did not move me into action.

I prayed for Hind to be found safe, for her to grow up in a free Palestine, and for a million beautiful futures to pour out of her like a steady stream of the prolific stardust that carries us Anishinaabeg. I prayed for her to have a descendant who, like me, would one day marvel at the strength of their ancestor who had endured so much so that they could be here. In those days, while the world waited with bated breath to hear what would happen to Hind, I prayed to my great-great-grandma to take care of Hind in those visceral moments of fear, to visit her somehow and give her reprieve.

But the Israeli army killed her, along with the paramedics who so selflessly went to save her, and I ruptured again.

I wish to say it out loud: Hind, Reem, Mahmoud, your martyrdom will ripple throughout generations of Anishinaabeg. Your martyrdom has touched our ancestors and beckoned them from the great beyond to come and usher in a new world. Hind, you joined my ancestors and bound me to my ancestral responsibilities. Reem, you called me back into my body and made me ready for action and sacrifice. Mahmoud, you ruptured me completely and made me understand that this moment demands new emotions, new dimensions of what it means to be a human being, of what it means to be Anishinaabe.

I imagine my great-great-grandma meeting Hind in the stars and greeting her. She holds her in her wise arms and little Hind feels peace. They laugh together and my ancestor tells Hind that many futures will pour out of her; some of them will even reach all the way to Turtle Island. They gaze at the earth below and watch these futures materialize in the bodies of whole and full Palestinians and Anishinaabeg. These are the ways that Native people are connected to the Palestinian struggle for liberation. It is not only through intellect or empathy or practicality; it is through our literal bodies and love-filled ancestors who live in the great beyond and call us into our collective responsibilities.

We must all become Hind's descendants, the people who will move mountains to create the world she deserved to live in, a material honouring of the struggle that so many children have lived and died through. A new world must come from her—this I insist.

And so, I imagine what it would look like and what it would feel like for my ancestors to stand beside the martyrs of Palestine. For Reem and Hind and Mahmoud, for every martyr, to stand beside my Anishinaabe ancestors who also suffered so greatly. My great-great-grandma embracing Hind, laughing together with stardust in their eyes. My great-grandfather, who has been with me so viscerally throughout all of this, taking Mahmoud gently in his arms, both their faces wrinkling into deep smiles. The courageous men of Palestine willing to sacrifice so much for their people, holding all the Anishinaabe babies who were stolen from us. And so, I paint this into reality.

The first time my daughter saw me openly sob about Palestine she met me with tender curiosity. Looking at me with her all-knowing eyes, she asked me if my heart was breaking, and when I nodded, she held me in her arms and stroked my head while I wept. She had just turned three. In Anishinaabe ways, children sit in the place before birth and see their entire lives, consenting to them when they choose their parents. They descend down the spider's silver thread with purpose and knowledge of the world they are entering. Our worldview lends us some semblance of comfort when our children are harmed or taken from the earth through settler colonial violence—the understanding that they were strong enough spirits to see their fate and choose it anyway, the unstoppable frothing of creation at the mouth of the great beyond.

It was clear to me that Giizik had come prepared for this moment. She had seen it in the stars, and I was here to learn from her. I would gaze at her sleeping toddler body and my heart would rupture for the children of Palestine in a way that moved me to action. I would overhear her from the next room saying, "Palestine will be free." In all the turmoil and pain, she held me in her focused stillness that anchored me to my responsibilities to build a better world for all children.

Parenting from an Anishinaabe understanding trusts in the gifts and medicines of our children to guide us through monumental hardships. All around me, parents were refusing to engage fully with Palestine on the basis of protecting their children, or protecting their normalcy for the sake of their children. In the imperial core, children are infantilized and depoliticized, rendered incapable of understanding the complex truths that govern our world, even though they are often the ones who suffer the brunt of its violence. Although it is true that children require boundaries around emotions and hard truths, I reject the complete infantilization of children that demands a sanitized reality for them. I also reject the compartmentalization of parenting to the ability to keep our children fed and healthy at the expense of our larger responsibilities to build a better world for them.

As I bore witness to the genocide in Gaza, I was changing so deeply, and of course my child was going to be a part of that. In fact, she taught me so much about how to live up to my responsibilities as an Anishinaabe parent and led the way for these changes to occur. In a way she could understand,

I told Giizik that children in Palestine don't have food or beds. She cried and we held each other. When I spoke at rallies, she was in the crowd, watching me. Later, I would watch her in her room pretending to speak at a rally, citing that we must keep the children safe, experimenting with the tone and loudness of her voice. When I went to organizing meetings, I would explain that I'm fighting for a better world for us and for Palestine. When I would miss a rally, she would cheekily ask me why I wasn't going to the "free, free Palestine" rally. When I co-lead a delegation of Palestinian organizers to come to Treaty 3 homelands, she was front and centre—as though she were the true mobilizer of this idea. And when I needed to rupture, I let myself cry in front of her. She held it all.

On a night in August 2024, I dreamed the thunderbirds came. They were blowing a storm so fierce across the land that they created a tsunami. I was with my Palestinian kin who had travelled to my homelands. We tried to run, but I could see the wave approaching. I looked up and felt complete despair because I was with Giizik. I told Giizik to hold her breath, but I knew she didn't know how. I held her tight in my arms, but I knew the force of the wave would separate us. There was nothing I could do as the wave approached. I believe I had been preparing for this dream for many months—the embodied feeling of what so many parents in Palestine carry every day. Complete helplessness as our children are taken from us. The wave swept us away, but we all survived. I looked around at Giizik and she was fine, and all my Palestinian kin were right beside me. When I woke up, I wept with this deep knowing and it shattered me. My identity as a parent is what lets me access this embodied empathy, a sacred tool to activate our sustained action.

Western parenting follows the principles of hierarchy and individualism. Within this framework, parenting becomes confined to how we contribute solely to our own child rather than how we contribute to the larger world that they inherit that includes the children of others. Fear is the tool that ontologically and physically confines us within these limitations. In a world of hyper-individualism and capitalism, we have been removed from our community support and understand that if we do not take care of our children, no one will. I came up against this fear. I felt vulnerable as a single mother who was carrying so much, knowing that it is not safe to challenge white supremacy and Zionism.

When I am scared to sacrifice my comfort and safety in this world, my capacity to imagine others doing the same is diminished and the world is a scary and hopeless place. When I am scared to extend my care to other children, I live in a world where I cannot imagine others caring for my child. Yet I decided to confront this fear. I realized that I had internalized the hierarchy and individualism of settler colonial society, and that all that separated me from the world I wanted to live in was fear.

When I decide that I am able to care for the children of the world with the same tenacity that I care for my own child, my child instantly becomes safer by virtue of the possibility of others doing the same. This is relationality. When I decide

I am able to sacrifice in order to fight for a better world, it instantly becomes the reality that other people are doing this, and the world becomes a more hopeful place. This is reciprocity. As soon as I made this transition in my mind, I felt a wave of relief. We create the worlds we want to live in, and in connecting my child and my sacrifices to others, I realized so much of the fear that we feel about safety, or lack thereof, is manufactured by settler colonialism. When we choose each other, we are powerful.

The only barrier between us and the collectivity we need to sustain our liberation and commitment to relationship-building, collaboration, and kinship is our manufactured fear. I have spent too much of my life nurturing my web of relationality to be indoctrinated into the individualism of the colonial world. We hold each other. We fight for each other's children. We sacrifice because we love. To be a good parent and to be Anishinaabe is to be willing to sacrifice for the worlds our children are helping us to create.

On our first night in the bush with our Palestinian kin on Treaty 3 homelands the mosquitos welcomed us with ferocity as we scrambled to set up our tents in the fading light. Despite the bugs, some of us hung the flag of Palestine at the water's edge that hummed a song of loving welcome. That night, the thunderbirds danced above us for hours. They shook the earth while the wind remained still, our humbled bodies lying below. For hours, they spoke to us of the rage and love of the universe, of how they had been summoned by the ripples of otherworldly violence that we cannot let persist.

Alongside my dear friend Tyanna Carpenter, an Anishinaabe organizer from Treaty 3, I coordinated a delegation of Palestinian organizers from the greater Toronto area to travel to Treaty 3 homelands. We did so in conversation with a broader organizing group of Palestinian and Indigenous organizers who had come together since the escalation of the genocide to build community and practices of joint struggle. We wanted to do something nation-specific, and we also wanted to offer the organizing landscape a piece of the work that was not being done—to move joint struggle into the realm of intimate, embodied kinship. We wanted to share our ceremonies with our Palestinian kin, whom we could see were at the brink of collapse and their own disembodiment. We wanted to share our homelands with our Palestinian kin, and let them be taken care of from our lands. We wanted our Elders to meet our Palestinian kin, and to share our stories of settler colonial violence and resistance so that we could better meet the current moment together.

We fundraised ferociously to fly fifteen participants from Toronto to Winnipeg to attend a one-week delegation that would traverse our beautiful homelands. We started with intensity, our first day spent attending ceremonies and being lucky enough to be shown birch bark scrolls that connect Anishinaabeg to Palestine and the far corners of the globe. We camped under the stars who watched us intently, and every single one of our animal relations came to greet us. During this delegation, we did many things. We built a lodge for our Elder. He extended our kinship and ceremonies to our Palestinian kin. People visited us and brought us cherished food and greetings. We visited my reserve of Lac des

Mille Lacs. Palestinians watched my brother in awe as he swam in the lake on our reserve for the first time. Our tears fell like the rain that followed us as the thunderbirds roared above, cloaking us in their otherworldly power and witnessing, and a tornado greeted us.

And it was Giizik who led us through all this monumental work—my little three-year-old wove us together in sacred silliness and love. Giizik was the glue that brought my mother, father, and brother on this trip. The last time my parents and I were at Lac des Mille Lacs was when I was a baby, cooing with the contentment of being on my homelands while they attempted to resist our forced displacement by building cabins on the reserve. Now, we all returned, this time to show our Palestinian kin the cabin I was building for my family and community—the circle of this work complete. Giizik was the one who brought my mother on this trip, insisting that she move beyond the inertia she had been grappling with in relation to taking action for Palestine. Giizik was the one who brought my father on this trip, inviting him to share our old, old stories from his grandparents as we drove through so many places he used to live. Giizik was the one who made my brother feel safe enough to come on this trip, lending the sacred playfulness of a child to an otherwise serious and overwhelming undertaking.

I witnessed Giizik on this trip with awe. It felt like she had orchestrated it all and was now in her element, the knowledge of the great beyond shining through her all-knowing eyes. She prayed at the foot of a tree for Palestine and the bears and the stars. She greeted our Elder like an old friend, tenderly embracing him for a long time. She knew exactly

when someone needed to be comforted, or when someone needed the ridiculously silly and nonsensical energy
of a toddler. It was like she had seen it all before, up in
those beautiful stars. At every rest stop, she would somehow acquire a sweet treat from every single Palestinian. She
had people playing under the table with her and laughing
deep in their bellies. And sometimes, she also ruptured. She
would scream and wail and contort her body, as toddlers
do, and we felt relief in her unbounded expression, longing
to do the same.

Giizik's presence on the delegation was also a visceral
reminder of what we are all fighting for—our children to
be free and whole, traversing their homelands, feeling safe
enough to be wild and playful, and respected as the knowl-
edgeable and medicine-filled beings they are. While we
showed Palestinians our homelands, we learned so much
from each other. I watched people play with my daughter
with presence and huge expressions of genuine joy and loud
love, and I felt healed from the ways our people have been
removed from our ability to do just that. Our Palestinian kin
taught us how to love again. In the shadow of the residential
school system, which stands just two generations away from
Giizik, she was teaching us all how to love louder, deeper,
and more expansively to bind our communities together
in kinship. As Anishinaabeg and Palestinian folks came
together on the land in grief and in deep commitment to
one another, the children helped us to be whole.

*Hind, what if you could have been there with us as we
traversed Treaty 3 homelands? I wonder how you would have*

played with my daughter. Would you have hidden under the table with her, convincing the adults to play silly games? How many sweet treats would you both have been able to acquire, shuffling from person to person, pretending you had none? I painted you in the stars, standing with my great-great-grandma, but I also painted iterations of you down below on the earth, children playing wild and free on Palestinian homelands whole and full.

Palestine taught me that our wholeness is deeply political, and it is our sacred responsibility to seek wholeness in order to achieve full liberation. To be whole is not to inherently feel good; to be whole is to reclaim our presence in everything that we are and everything we are connected to. We need to be able to glimpse our expansive embodiment for our full liberation, and there are so many ways to get there. Beyond the colonial fear, beyond the compartmentalizations of body from land, we dance within our webs of creation wildly and with the tenacity of creation that will allow us to build the world we dream.

Palestine called me back to my body, demanding that I be embodied in order to build the world we so urgently need. When the genocide escalated, the smoke inside my body began to swirl so loudly that all I could do was move with it. Through my embodiment, I was able to be in direct conversation with my ancestors and spirit kin, who were similarly activated by the violence echoing across the universe. The smoke of my daughter's body began to swirl, and the spider who still binds her to the great beyond began to weave a new web of Anishinaabeg and Palestinian wholeness bound as one. I was finally able to put paintbrush to canvas again, and I painted a future where our ancestors and martyrs witness our inevitable wholeness. My daughter showed me how to make this real—Anishinaabeg and Palestinian kin dancing across Treaty 3 homelands, full of grief but working to be whole, perhaps disembodied but glimpsing holy embodiment.

I imagine them in the starry sky, standing beside one another—all my ancestors and all of Palestine's martyrs. There are so many children. There are so many babies. My great-great-grandma is standing with Hind. My great-grandpa Pete is holding Mahmoud in his arms. Reem is smiling so brightly because her grandfather stands by her side. In this otherworldly moment, our ancestors and martyrs gather to see us down below in the future, full and whole. They see Palestinian and Anishinaabe children who don't know harm or hurt, bellies full, laughter echoing throughout the universe that makes the thunderbirds weep with happiness. They see Palestinian and Anishinaabe Elders growing old on their homelands, the grief in their hearts healed every day by the freedom of their children. They see the beautiful future of the work we all must do. They see what will be.

Our wholeness will usher in the world we have been dreaming

I can feel the smoke inside me now, in every waking moment of every day. Alive and agentive, it slowly churns stardust through my blood, and my body becomes a constellation that lights my way home. Sometimes, the smoke is a whisper. Sometimes, the smoke is my ancestors talking to me through the ethereal fog of the great beyond. Sometimes, the smoke is the trembling universe begging us to witness so that we may build a new world. Always, the smoke is a boundless and transcendent love that persists beyond time and space, beyond this body and the next. We are always everything and so far beyond.

Our wholeness, however momentary and fleeting, is irrevocably ours. Tucked deep within the flesh of our bodies and rooted in bones that have grown to hold so much, the swirling smoke connects us to all that we are and all that we will be. No matter how much violence our bodies endure, how far we travel away from our bodies in order to survive, or how much harm we witness come to the people we love, the smoke remains. Our ancestors work tirelessly to keep our embers warm, making tea and chuckling with each other as the smoke rises to tickle the stars that so adore us. Our spirit kin visit us through our smoke, taking brief form as they brush against our flesh to remind us of our purpose that lives in the place beyond time. Our homelands hold us through our smoke, our bodies leaving a soft imprint in their warm embrace. To be whole is to be held by our bodies and all they contain, the flowing tendrils of creation wrapping our spirits in the deep relationality that is our inherent right.

Before I had a body, I swirled like smoke throughout the vast universe. I joined the low moan of creation with my rumbling breath, a symphony of vibratory sounds that pulsed throughout the universe, the sound of a black hole. Sometimes, I was the collective smoke swirling around the eddies of the pink and sparkling universe, my essence dissolved into an incomprehensible plurality. Sometimes, I was summoned and became more discrete in my form, ushering the smoke to become a river that would travel to where I was needed. In the place beyond body, I cared for and loved my descendants so tenderly, sometimes becoming the whisper that would calm them in the night, smoke rising in their bellies.

In the place beyond body, I sat with many creatures of the universe to weave together futures that would be birthed below. In the place beyond body, I swirled like smoke throughout the vast universe and I was whole because I was *the* whole.

Before I was born, I was summoned to the place before birth. The magenta smoke that held me took the form of a long and winding snake that travelled to meet my ancestors who waited for me at the precipice of time. I gazed upon the world below—all the pain and all the suffering of the beings I was connected to, all the ruptures and violence that would exist during my lifetime, all the loss and all the grief that would envelop my human body—and I still chose to descend. I saw my parents and their entire lives—all their suffering and turmoil—and I chose them. I saw my own body and what it would carry—all its breaches and erosion—and I chose me. I nodded to the spider who weaves children to the earth, and the spider spun the sparkling thread that would lead me to my body.

All the blood, all the tears, all the numbness, and all the loss of the world could never keep me from delighting in the sweetness of creation. All the pain and all the suffering could never keep me from the exuberance of being alive and living out my responsibilities to build better worlds that will echo throughout the vast and loving universe.

I have to imagine this choice exists for all children. Children of the world who bear the brunt of so much violence, I have to believe that you saw your fate and decided to come anyway. Children of the world who bear the brunt of colonialism and empire, I have to believe that you carry that strong and old medicine to be a spirit who can endure a cruel fate because you understand that you are so much more than this moment. Children of the world, our keepers of hope and messengers of the great beyond, I have to believe that we will create the world that will keep you here and hold you while you grow old. Our love is a testament to our spiritual persistence that, again and again, in sacred perpetuity, chooses to delight in our fleeting humanity before we once again return to our loving kin of the universe.

When I was born, I met the confines of my physical body. My vibrating form was encased within the boundaries of skin and the limitations of linear time, but my mother was there to greet me. She held me on her chest, and my brother looked at me with the same adoration that the stars gaze upon us with. My father was there with a goofy, wrinkled smile, and my grandmother wrapped me in her big fur coat on that cold day in January. In an instant, I was reunited with so many that I love. In a moment, my swirling smoke now lived in a body that was firmly planted in the here and now. In a sudden flash of light, I found myself to be a discrete entity who would now experience the world through a body. My skin was tight, like an enforced stillness around the hum of the great beyond that still rippled through me. My limbs felt foreign, like learning how to control something external. But I also felt delight. My body was holding me in place so that I could experience the here and now. I pressed my body into the warmth of my mother's and basked in the elation of my new humanity.

My body, like the bodies of so many others, was born into the settler colonial world. This world is one of rigidity and control, manufactured through sharp violence. As I grew, I encountered harm and loss that eroded my body, bits and pieces of me falling off. As I grew, I encountered the imposed stillness of my body through the infrastructure of settler colonialism that attempts to hold me in place, compressing my body. As a child, I witnessed disembodiment in the people around me as a way to survive these conditions. And so, I learned how to do the same. Slowly travelling away from my body, I began to disembody myself so that I could experience relief from the erosion and compression of my body in the settler colonial bog. At times, I could not find my body at all, and I wailed into the cold, dark, and empty night.

But despite my disembodiment, I always found ways to spill over. Our disembodiment could never keep us from our inherent wholeness. The swirling smoke always remained inside my body and called me home when I could not find my body in the cold night. When I was a young girl, I painted worlds that spat in the face of settler colonialism, and I wrote poetry that celebrated the great beyond. When I was a young woman, I helped young people feel the swirling smoke inside their bodies, even when I could not grow closer to my own body. I placed my body on my homelands and challenged my disembodiment, working toward my ability to be present within my body such that my wholeness could hold me. I visualized wholeness through painting my body in pleasure and expansive relationality.

When I was twenty-eight, my body ruptured with stardust and blood and sacred water as my daughter descended that same spider's thread to meet me. She taught me how to be whole, and how to protect her wholeness through my desire to be present in my own body.

When I was thirty-one, I was called to radical embodiment by the people of Palestine, the collective grief of the genocide demanding my wholeness in order to fight urgently for a new world. I began to understand that tending to the sacred smoke inside me is not just a pathway to my own freedom and fullness but a responsibility to fight for collective liberation.

I lie in my bed as my body fills with grief. The grief of my spirit, the grief of my ancestors, the grief of the entire universe wells up in my body, and I might burst. It is unbearable, yet this is what has called me to be embodied. My ability to feel this collective grief is carried into my body through the swirling smoke of the great beyond. My ability to feel this collective grief is only possible because I am whole. To become whole for another is a beautiful thing. Maybe this is one of our pathways forward. When we cannot desire complete and absolute wholeness for ourselves, we can find the will to fight for our wholeness for others. We are only able to sacrifice and bleed for the worlds we must build when we are whole.

Our wholeness might be momentary and fleeting, but it is important that we know it is within us, in absolution. In the settler colonial world of unimaginable violence, it feels nearly impossible to be truly whole until the infrastructure of violence is dismantled. Although Palestine called me back into my body for a remarkably long period of time, I eventually confronted the limits of withstanding the pain of being fully present in an Indigenous body. Now, I continue to lapse between varied states of presence within my body. But importantly, I dance with the swirling smoke inside of me more frequently now, and I better understand the pathways that allow me to be embodied—splashing colour across the canvas that sings a vision of a beautiful future, living a life of joy and pleasure in my body as an Indigenous woman so that my daughter can inherit my wholeness, gazing into the stardust of my daughter's eyes and feeling the radiating love of the great beyond, realizing that even our pain and grief can render us whole as we stand firmly in our bodies to channel creation's demands for a better world. It is our desire for wholeness that is the pathway to our liberation.

Working toward wholeness is not just the inherent right of Indigenous peoples, but the right of every single human being and entity of creation. The global scaffolding of empire and its tentacles of settler colonialism seek to render every single person fragmented and removed from their expansive web of relationality in order to support the individualism, hierarchy, and control that is at the centre of empire. For this reason, the ontological foundation of settler colonialism is the compartmentalization of body from expansive creation. The ontological foundation of settler colonialism is the compartmentalization of all facets of life—to render us incapable of embodying our inherent wholeness.

The forces of settler colonialism must break us all into bits and pieces so that we cannot rely on the collectivity of creation. They must break us all into bits and pieces so that we tolerate vapid and hollow lives within capitalism. They must break us all into bits and pieces so that we feel nothing and do nothing when they do the same to others. Whether we are broken through blood and violence, or enticed into breaking ourselves apart through privilege and power, empire can only function with broken human beings.

Every single person has a web of creation. While yours may not be the same as mine—the specific stars that I come from, the manoomin blowing gently in the waters of

Treaty 3, the muskrat I am bound to through clan, and the bears that guard my tenderness—it is undoubtedly just as expansive. Creation wills it to be so. Insist on a life where you are convening in responsibility with the entirety of your web of creation—the homelands that you come from, the homelands that you may occupy, your ancestors who might be begging you to listen to them, your children who need your sacrifice in order to build a better world, your neighbours, the nations across the globe experiencing genocide, the people who might be oppressed because of your specific privileges, the honourable moon, the beating sun, and your own thirsty spirit.

Reclaiming our wholeness is not an idyllic and romanticized process of appropriating the Anishinaabe worldview I have presenced within this book, but rather it is a commitment to material sacrifice and responsibility oriented toward the collective. To be whole is to be able to feel the buckling weight of imperial violence, bloodshed, and loss, and to commit to the sacrifice of your privilege, power, comfort, normalcy, and body in order to live out your true and expansive responsibilities as a human being.

I can feel the smoke inside me now, and it makes me feel so full. I can't imagine a more beautiful reality than to be willing to sacrifice for those outside myself. I can't imagine a more transcendent existence than to be so cherished by creation that it continues to whisper sweet visions of the future into my ears. I can't imagine a more righteous love than to be held by my ancestors who have invented ways to dance with me throughout the human experience. Nothing can ever touch

our smoke. Despite the violence, despite the harms, despite
the suffering, our smoke is otherworldly in its sovereignty.
They can never contain the smoke; us Anishinaabeg always
spill over. They can never reach the smoke; it evades every
grasp. We are everything they can never contain.

I dance with my body in all its broken complexity. I cherish the smoke inside me, and ebb and flow with the tides of presence and disembodiment that sustain me in this messy settler colonial world. I chart pathways to our collective and permanent wholeness—pathways to our inevitable liberation—understanding what allows me to swirl wildly with the smoke inside my body.

I dance with my beautiful daughter and all her inherent wholeness. The smoke inside us rises to the stars she took me to visit in my dream, singing a song of how she will always find me in this universe in order to love me in many forms.

I dance with my mother, insisting on my wholeness so that it may spill onto her. I dance with my father, holding him as a small child before he was taken away to residential school so that he can feel loved before the storm.

I dance with Hind through my great-great-grandmother, filling her up with the joy of knowing that a free Palestine will come from her. I dance with all our small and beautiful children taken through imperial violence, the children I have watched pass away on my phone, the children in the mass graves across Turtle Island, the children across the world who bear the brunt of colonial and imperial violence. They comfort me for they are those old and ancient spirits who carry the deepest medicine of the expansive universe, and their sacrifice is a drop of water in an expansive ocean of their complete and utter wholeness. They whisper that we all will soon be whole.

I dance with my ancestors whose laughter echoes throughout the great beyond. Kakekayatahseekobiik—never-ending light. That is my name. Creation is always frothing at the mouth of the great beyond. Kakekayatahseekobiik—that which feels lost always remains, in me. That which feels lost always remains, in us.

Acknowledgements

I am still incredulous that I have, in fact, finished this book. It has been such a long journey because life is always hard and complicated and tender and breathtaking. When I first started writing this book, my daughter was two years old, and now she is almost five. This book has been written for more than half of her beautiful life. I do not recognize myself from the start of this work, and of that I am proud. I have transformed. My daughter has transformed. My life has transformed. It is all of our responsibilities to transform wildly in order to meet the world with justice and goodness and wholeness.

Miigwech, first and foremost, to the reader for making it this far. I hope that some of my words can be a part of our collective transformation into better worlds. And now I look forward to letting these words go. Words I have analyzed and sutured together can now simply be.

It is hard for me to separate my acknowledgements related specifically to this book from the other aspects of my life over the past three years. My acknowledgements are thus expansive—I wish to honour not only those who explicitly helped me with this book but also those who held me during this time in numerous ways.

Miigwech to my support system and closest sisters, Salia Joseph and Keisha Charnley, who read random parts of this book in our disjointed, comedic, omnipresent, and nonsensical group chat. Our relationships truly make me who I am, and I am so honoured to walk beside you both in this lifetime. I am in awe of you as friends, sisters, mothers, and worldbuilders.

Miigwech to my family, who touch this book deeply and are woven throughout, but particularly to my mother, Nerine Christie; my father, Ronald Momogeeshik Peters; my brothers Malqalm and Mitchell Peters; and my sister, Nylah Christie-Smith. Miigwech to my family who were beside me when I wrote the very first chapter of this book in Thunder Bay in our Parsons house—Kaitlyn Adams, Casha Adams, Mary Lou Adams. Miigwech to my grandmother, always and in so many ways, Agnes Kabatay.

Miigwech to my wonderful editor, Shirarose Wilensky, who pushed me to deeply consider the intention behind my words, and who accepted my convictions as an Anishinaabe person writing non-linearly and from a cultural rootedness. It is so important to have editors who believe in work that is in tension with mainstream writing, so thank you for championing this book into something we are both incredibly proud of. And miigwech to the amazing folks at House of Anansi for supporting this work, and to Alysia Shewchuk for the beautiful design work surrounding the cover.

Miigwech to my team of community readers who so generously offered their perspectives on this work. Miigwech to Erin Konsmo, who provided tremendous feedback for some of my blindspots in the initial manuscript. Thank you for doing the work of building a world that is gentler for all people. Miigwech to Maysam Abu Khreibeh for being my hype man, and for offering such meaningful reflections on this work, particularly the chapter about Palestine. I'm in adoration of you and the work that you do to bring our communities together, always. Miigwech to Melody McIver, Jacky Deng, Caolan Barr, and Willow Crow for reading my words and being a part of this initial sharing. I am normally a private and insular creator who likes to share my creations only once they are near perfect. Thank you to everyone for being part of a new type of vulnerability for me.

Miigwech to my Elder and dear friend Al Hunter, who does so much for our community, and who has also been the beacon of light and guidance as we do the work to bring Palestinian community members to Treaty 3 territory. You are so full of love, and we love you so much. Chii miigwech for all the work you do to lead Anishinaabeg into wholeness. Words truly fail here.

Miigwech to my dear friend and collaborator Tyanna Carpenter, who found me in the settler colonial storm so that we could live out our deepest responsibilities as Anishinaabeg. Becoming kin with you has felt deeply spiritual, and I am constantly in awe of you. Glimpsing your inner world through our friendship feels like home and keeps me going.

Miigwech to Alanah Astehtsi' Otsistóhkwa' Jewell for being on this wonderful journey with me as a friend. Miigwech to Pavel Volgarev for providing such tender support while Giizik and I moved through a life transition and this book. Miigwech to Lisa Bellamy for helping me with my daughter so that I could attend rallies and do my organizing work, and for being so affirming when times were hard. Miigwech to my cousin Jana-Rae Yerxa for always holding it down in Treaty 3 with such love and strength for our people. Miigwech to my dear friend Shabina Lafleur-Gangji for all the critical conversations we had amid the chatter of our kids playing in utter joyful chaos.

Last but not least, miigwech to my friend and collaborator Kristen Bos, who helped me navigate the process of writing a book when I had no idea what I was doing, and who rooted me so firmly in the certainty of my convictions as an Anishinaabe writer. You are so incredibly selfless and truly live to lift everyone up around you, materially and with ferocity. Here's to our future collaborative children's book about toots, which we undoubtedly need after the seriousness of the books we both just wrote.

And finally, chii miigwech to my universe, my centre, the entire reason for this book, the invocator of our collective wholeness, the future unfolding: Giizik Hiinu Funmaker-Peters. So much of the knowledge within this book comes from her brilliance, not in a tokenistic way but in a literal way. I gaze into the great beyond every day in her piercing eyes. She moves me to action. Miigwech for being my greatest teacher. Miigwech for finding me again within the expanse of this unfolding universe. I will always choose lifetimes with you, infinitely and without pause. It is my greatest delight to know you and love you. I will always choose lifetimes with you.

QUILL CHRISTIE-PETERS is an Anishinaabe educator and self-taught visual artist from Lac des Mille Lacs First Nation located in Treaty 3 territory. She is the creator and director of the Indigenous Youth Residency Program, an artist residency for Indigenous youth that engages land-based creative practices through Anishinaabe artistic methodologies. She holds a master's degree in Indigenous governance on Anishinaabe art-making as a process of falling in love. She has spoken at Stanford University, the University of Toronto, and California College of the Arts, and her written work can be found in *GUTS* magazine and *Canadian Art*. She is also a mother, beadwork artist, organizer, and traditional tattoo practitioner following the protocols of her community. All of her work can be found at @raunchykwe.